Scrap School

12 ALL-NEW DESIGNS FROM AMAZING QUILTERS

LISSA ALEXANDER

Martingale®
Create with Confidence

Scrap School: 12 All-New Designs from Amazing Quilters
© 2021 by Lissa Alexander

Martingale®
18939 120th Ave. NE, Ste. 101
Bothell, WA 98011-9511 USA
ShopMartingale.com

Printed in Hong Kong
26 25 24 23 22 21   8 7 6 5 4 3 2 1

Library of Congress Cataloging-in-Publication Data is available upon request.

ISBN: 978-1-68356-118-7

MISSION STATEMENT

We empower makers who use fabric and yarn to make life more enjoyable.

CREDITS

PUBLISHER AND CHIEF VISIONARY OFFICER
Jennifer Erbe Keltner

CONTENT DIRECTOR
Karen Costello Soltys

DESIGN MANAGER
Adrienne Smitke

TECHNICAL EDITOR
Nancy Mahoney

PRODUCTION MANAGER
Regina Girard

TECHNICAL WRITER
Martha Gamm

PHOTOGRAPHERS
Adam Albright
Brent Kane

COPY EDITOR
Melissa Bryan

ILLUSTRATOR
Sandy Loi

SPECIAL THANKS
Photography for this book was taken at the home of Libby Warnken of Ankeny, Iowa.

DEDICATION

To teachers everywhere. I have had some incredible teachers along the way, and at the time I had no idea how those lessons would prepare me for my future. So whether you're a math teacher, a quilt teacher, or a constant learner, I hope you enjoy the lessons in Scrap School.

Contents

Welcome to Scrap School

As I write this book, we are going through a worldwide pandemic; people are staying at home, and yet the sewing community is growing by leaps and bounds. Quilters are using their stashes, doing online swaps, and turning to the art of quiltmaking as therapy. Whether you make any of the quilts in this book from a curated fabric collection, your treasured scraps, or from only two fabric colors, my hope is that your takeaway from these pages will be a study guide to color placement, and that you'll learn more about how to create movement through the quilt by the use of color or quilting choices. I also hope you gain the freedom to play with your scraps.

Most people have a particular style and work within that style or a favored color family. I, on the other hand, tend to enjoy all sorts of styles. Nothing in my house matches—or maybe my style could be described as eclectic. In short, I love fabric and am obsessed with color. While working at Moda Fabrics I have the opportunity to play with different designers' lines, but when sewing for myself, I like to combine fabric collections. To build my own color confidence I start with Moda precuts. I like to work in reds, whites, and blues; green and reds; or a combination of oranges, melons, plums, and purples. This pretty much covers all the holiday or seasonal quilts—and don't even get me started on how much I love a rainbow palette.

I invited ten other designers whose quilts and styles I admire to join me in creating quilts for *Scrap School*. They don't all see things the way I do, so it not only broadens the variety you'll find in this book, but it also offers the opportunity for each of us to learn more about what makes a good scrap quilt, and what makes each of the individual quilts special.

Whether you prefer a more planned scrap quilt or color palette, or you love a scrap quilt that has dozens or even hundreds of fabrics, you're sure to find inspiration in these pages. Let's start by learning a bit about a wonderful group of scrap-quilt designers I call the *Scrap School* staff and the way they plan their scrap quilts. School is in session!

~ Lissa

Let's Look at Scrappy Color Palettes

Just as I did in *Sisterhood of Scraps* (Martingale, 2020), I wanted to share with you a wide variety of scrap quilts in styles by various designers, not just me. So once again, I've invited quilters I admire to be part of this book. Some of these quilters I've known personally for years and some I've never met. But they all have one thing in common—they all create beautiful quilts that I love, and I'm pretty sure you will too. I think looking at the work of a variety of different designers to see how they go about creating a beautiful scrap quilts expands the concept of scrap quilting for all of us (myself included).

Two of the designers who are known to me for their style are **Lisa Bongean** of Primitive Gatherings and **Sherri McConnell** of A Quilting Life. Lisa and Sherri each designed a quilt using scraps from several of their Moda fabric lines. These curated fabric lines are designed to work well together, so even if you use 30 or more fabrics, the result will be cohesive. A good tip is that if you love a certain Moda designer, then you should have great success mixing fabrics from several of their lines. A designer's fabric line is a good starting point for successful color and scale; then you can make it your own by adding additional fabrics from your scraps.

I have included swatch cards from Lisa Bongean's Scrappy Dots and Dashes quilt with the fabrics arranged by color (see page 7), but the main thing I wanted to point out is that you should always consider a fabric's overprint. Lisa's quilt uses almost-identical reds as a base color, but you'll see that one red has a black print and another has a sparse tan print; this creates a completely different density of color. Lisa used them together with great results.

I am so honored to have **Connie Tesene and Mary Etherington** of Country Threads join us on "staff" at *Scrap School*. They have been huge influences on my quilting life. I've made many of their patterns, visited their farm, and even did a little two-step dancing in their barn (but that's a different story). I have to attribute my love of scrappiness to Connie and Mary. They were the first ones to teach me it was OK to use a wide range of fabrics in a single quilt.

The Country Threads design team, known for their farmhouse style, has created a combination of traditional Star and Log Cabin quilt blocks in Sea Glass Stars on page 27. But they pumped up their color selection by using aqua, teals, grays, and a pop of cheddar/orange, all atop light background prints. The main prints seem to do all the work in the design and they did not need to use a large variety of prints to make this happen, but it's their use of colorful mid-scale, low-volume (light) background prints that make all those other colors work so well.

Much like Connie and Mary have influenced me, so has **Susan Ache.** Susan's eye for color is impeccable and she always adds a touch whimsy (or maybe that is just her personality showing through). Susan looks at patterns in a completely different way than I do and incorporates a sense of classic color. If you're a social-media fan, you'll want to follow Susan (@Yardgrl60) on Instagram to see more of her inspiring quilts and color combinations.

Sarah Huechteman has got to be one of the busiest gals I know. She works fulltime at an elementary school, teaches classes at a quilt shop, and sews for Moda Fabrics and various magazines (including *American Patchwork and Quilting*) creating color options. Sarah's quilt, While at Lunch (page 63), is perfectly named since that's probably the only time she was able to work on it. Thank you, Sarah, for making time for this in your busy schedule. (To see the *real* story behind the name for this quilt, see page 63.)

Sarah's palette is bold, with aqua and gray as the main colors. The shapes in her pattern are large, so you could get away with choosing larger-scale prints while keeping the background prints small. Mixing the darks and lights makes the design pop with secondary designs. Take a look at the swatch cards for While at Lunch (page 8) to explore scale and pattern.

Amanda Jean Nyberg of Crazy Mom Quilts and **Amy Smart** of A Diary of a Quilter both designed quilts that are great examples of fun, festive rainbow palettes. Simple repeated shapes make the sewing easy and let the fabric do all the work. In Amanda's quilt (Two-Step on page 49), it's as if the Crayola Ultimate Color Collection box of 152 crayons spilled out on the fabrics. The prints are colorful and for the most part they're tone-on-tones with just a touch of color sprinkled on them, making each

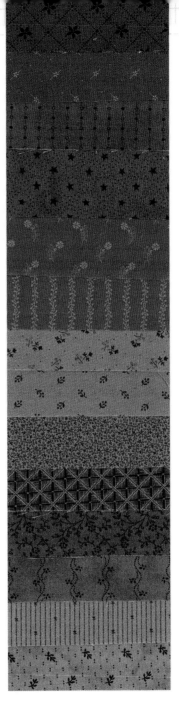
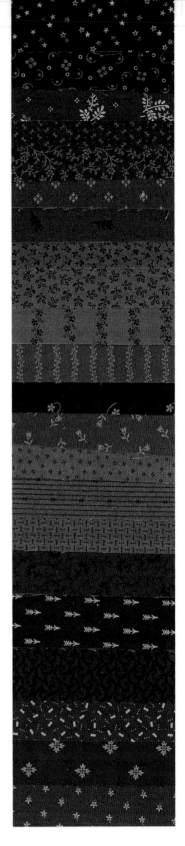

Swatches from Lisa Bongean's Scrappy Dots and Dashes on page 21.

Swatches for Sarah Huechteman's While at Lunch on page 63.

patchwork square stand on its own. Have you ever Googled "colors of the rainbow" to arrange fabric color flow? I have. My interpretation of her swatch palette is shown on page 9.

In Country Fair on page 43, Amy used fewer fabrics and paid attention to prints with lots of color. She concentrated on consistency in the backgrounds, sashing squares, and borders. The red border frames the design, creating a sense of depth. Whether you are using 152 fabrics or your favorite 25 fabrics, the results will be pleasing when you follow the rainbow.

Do you squint when making quilts? I do all the time to focus on the value placement and not just color. In particular, I squinted when I saw **Gudrun Erla's** Spin Cycle (page 55) and when I was designing my own quilt Rolling Nine Patches (page 12). Gudrun's quilt uses sophisticated background fabrics with navy blue squares that create a circular pattern and feature a large background print. This is a great design to showcase a main signature print that is not normally used in scrap quilts.

Rolling Nine Patches has a huge range of fabrics, and I admit, not all of the fabrics used were mine. It started as a nine-patch swap with Sandy Klop of American Jane and her friends. I love making quilts that have a secondary pattern that makes them look much harder than they are. Gudrun used a repeat block with half-blocks to create circular movement in her design. Rolling Nine Patch is pieced as a block with additional sashing that actually creates the design. Both of these quilts offer an excellent opportunity to let the quilting create additional movement or accentuate the circular spins in the patchwork designs.

While many of the quilts in this book build from a simple square or rectangle, **Kim Diehl's** Please and Thank You quilt (page 89) and my Hidden Blocks quilt (page 83) have created their own kind of movement with the use of triangles. One fun thing that scrap quilts do is create a game for the eye. Using many colors, prints, and textures makes your eye travel throughout the design, and then mixing in the angles that triangles bring almost makes it like viewing a tennis match or a ping-pong game. Study the fabric placement of the mediums and darks while coloring the same pattern differently to win in the overall design. While these two quilts use very different blocks, another thing to pay attention to is the difference between blocks set on point and blocks that are set straight. Blocks set on point often look more interesting because they create additional movement in the design, sending your eye from edge to edge.

If you love one of the color swatches shown, feel free to dive in and use it to make any of the quilts. And be sure to look at all the quilts and color options throughout the book as a way to study color and design. But most importantly, feel free to experiment along the way.

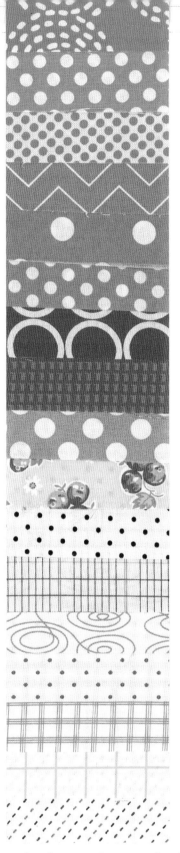

*Swatches for Amanda Jean Nyberg's
Two-Step quilt on page 49.*

Meet the Scrap-School Staff

LISA BONGEAN

I call Lisa the **Master of Micro Piecing** because she loves creating small patchwork with lots of fabrics. She does some sort of stitching every day, and her mantra is, "The more fabrics in a quilt, the better the quilt is." As scrap quilters, I think we can all agree with that! *PrimitiveGatherings.us*

CONNIE TESENE AND MARY ETHERINGTON

Connie and Mary, **Professors of the More the Merrier,** started their pattern business, Country Threads, in 1982, after discovering their mutual love of design. They self-published books and patterns and opened their famous quilt shop on Mary's farm near Garner, Iowa.

AMANDA JEAN NYBERG

Amanda Jean, **Supervisor of No Scrap Left Unsewn,** is a scrap quilter to the core. Since beginning quilting in 2000, she's completed nearly 350 quilts! She is an author and is constantly looking for new and innovative ways to turn scraps into beautiful finished objects. *CrazyMomQuilts.blogspot.com*

SUSAN ACHE

Susan undoubtedly has her **PhD of Scrappy Blocks.** This mom of five grown children lives in Florida, where local scenery is the color source for her quilts. With so many fabric options out there, she doesn't see her creative journey ending for a long time! *@yardgrl60*

KIM DIEHL

Kim is admired by thousands of quilters for her series of "Simple" quilting books. After chancing upon a pattern book at a sidewalk sale, Kim taught herself how to sew quilts and entered and won a national contest with the third quilt she'd ever made, which propelled her to **Head of Graduate Studies in Corralling Scraps!** *@kim_diehl_quilts*

SHERRI L. McCONNELL

Inspired by a family heritage of women who love sewing and creating, Sherri began quilting as a young mom. In 2008, this **Counselor of Containing Scraps** started her quilting blog, *AQuiltingLife.com,* and soon began publishing patterns, writing quilting books, and designing fabrics for Moda with her daughter Chelsi Stratton.

SARAH HUECHTEMAN

Sarah is a part-time fabric peddler and teacher at her local quilt shop. I call her the **Principal of Getting Things Done** because she is always busy and never misses a deadline. Sarah says, "I was super excited to join with this wonderful group of designers—some that I know and some that I'm in awe of!" *@sarahhuechteman*

GUDRUN ERLA

Gudrun, who in this book is the **Administrator of Big-Print Scrap Quilts,** was born and raised in Iceland. After owning and running quilt shops there, quilting drew her to Minnesota, where she now lives and designs quilts, rulers, and notions for her company, GE Designs. *GEQuiltDesigns.com*

AMY SMART

Amy, our resident **Fellow of Freeing Up Your Scrap Bin,** is a wife, mom, quilter, and fabric lover living in her native state of Utah. Amy's also an author, teacher, and fabric designer for Riley Blake Designs. *DiaryofaQuilter.com*

Lisa

Connie & Mary

Amanda

Susan

Kim

Sherri

Sarah

Gudrun

Amy

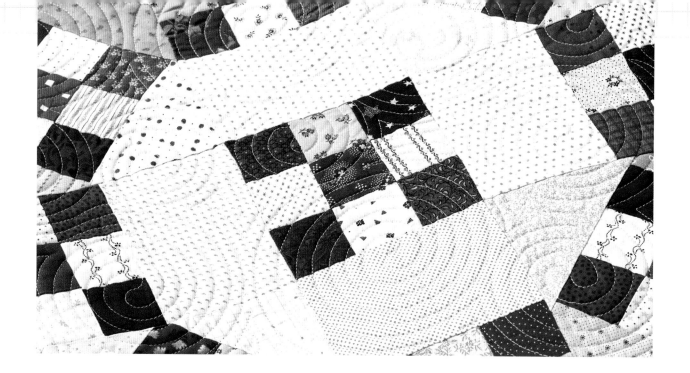

ROLLING NINE PATCHES

Designed and pieced by Lissa Alexander; quilted by Maggi Honeyman

Nine Patches are great blocks to make using leftover bits and pieces from other projects. Here they go 'round and 'round but let me share my secret: there's not a single curve in this quilt. It's all straight seams. You'll be on a roll piecing the cleverly assembled patchwork and sashing.

FINISHED QUILT: 80½" × 100½"

FINISHED BLOCK: 15½" × 15½"

Materials

Yardage is based on 42"-wide fabric.

- 8½ yards of assorted light prints for blocks and sashing

- 3⅜ yards of assorted red prints for blocks and sashing

- ⅞ yard of dark red print for binding

- 7½ yards of fabric for backing

- 89" × 109" piece of batting

Cutting

All measurements include ¼" seam allowances.

From the assorted red prints, cut a *total* of:
49 strips, 2" × 42"; crosscut into 98 strips, 2" × 21"

From the dark red print, cut:
10 strips, 2½" × 42"

Continued on page 14

Continued from page 12

From the assorted light prints, cut a *total* of:

40 strips, 2" × 42"; crosscut into 80 strips, 2" × 21" (1 is extra)

6 strips, 4½" × 42"; crosscut into 42 squares, 4½" × 4½". Cut the squares in half diagonally to yield 84 small triangles.

6 strips, 8" × 42"; crosscut into 28 squares, 8" × 8". Cut the squares into quarters diagonally to yield 112 large triangles.

10 strips, 3¾" × 42"; crosscut into 80 rectangles, 3¾" × 5"

25 strips, 2⅜" × 42"; crosscut into:
   48 rectangles, 2⅜" × 5"
   90 rectangles, 2⅜" × 7¼"
   4 rectangles, 2⅜" × 9"

Making the Blocks

Press all seam allowances as indicated by the arrows.

1. Sew red 2" × 21" strips to each long side of a light strip to make a strip set. Make 39 strip sets measuring 5" × 21", including seam allowances. Cut the strip sets into cut 384 segments, 2" × 5".

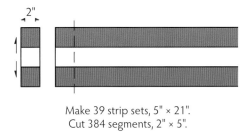

Make 39 strip sets, 5" × 21".
Cut 384 segments, 2" × 5".

2. Sew light strips to each long side of a red 2" × 21" strip to make a strip set. Make 20 strip sets measuring 5" × 21", including seam allowances. Cut the strip sets into 192 segments, 2" × 5".

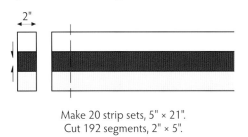

Make 20 strip sets, 5" × 21".
Cut 192 segments, 2" × 5".

3. Join two segments from step 1 and one segment from step 2 to make a nine-patch unit. Make 192 units measuring 5" square, including seam allowances.

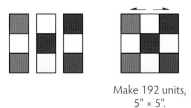

Make 192 units,
5" × 5".

4. Lay out three nine-patch units, two light 2⅜" × 5" rectangles, and two light small triangles. Join the pieces to make a center strip. Make one strip for each block (12 total).

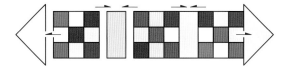

Make 1 strip per block (12 total).

5. Join two light 2⅜" × 7¼" rectangles and one light 2⅜" × 5" rectangle as shown to make a sashing strip measuring 2⅜" × 18½", including seam allowances. Make two strips for each block (24 total).

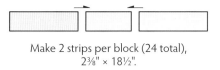

Make 2 strips per block (24 total),
2⅜" × 18½".

6. Join two light large triangles, one light small triangle, and one nine-patch unit to make a corner unit. Make two units per block (24 total).

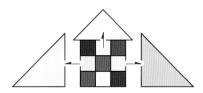

Make 2 units per block (24 total).

Lissa's Scrap School Tip

If red isn't your thing, make this quilt using an assortment of reproduction fabrics or even solids would be yummy. If you don't have enough scraps of your preferred colorway, expand your library of fabrics by participating in a block exchange. It's a great way to acquire more fabrics, and to make new friends!

7. Join one center strip, two sashing strips, and two corner units, making sure to align the seams, to make a center block. Note that the pieces are oversized and will be trimmed in the next step. Make 12 blocks.

8. Trim each block, making sure to leave ¼" seam allowance beyond the points of all the nine-patch units. The blocks should measure 16" square, including seam allowances.

Make 12 center blocks.

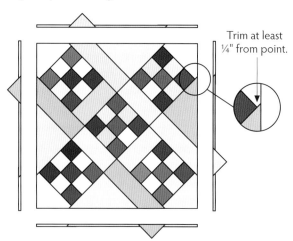

Trim at least ¼" from point.

Trim each block to 16" × 16".

Making the Corner and Half Blocks

1. Join one nine-patch unit, two light small triangles, two light large triangles, and one light 2⅜" × 9" rectangle. Make four corner blocks.

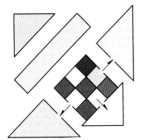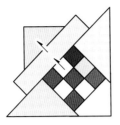

Make 4 corner blocks.

2. Trim each corner block, making sure to leave ¼" seam allowance beyond the points of the nine-patch unit along the right and bottom edges. The blocks should measure 8¼" square, including seam allowances.

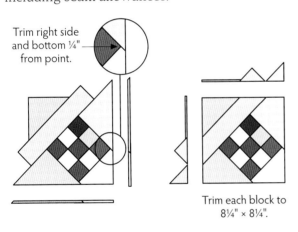

Trim right side and bottom ¼" from point.

Trim each block to 8¼" × 8¼".

3. Join one nine-patch unit, one light small triangle, and two light large triangles. Make 14 units.

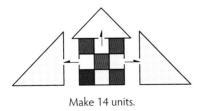

Make 14 units.

4. Join two light 2⅜" × 7¼" rectangles. Make 14 units measuring 2⅜" × 14".

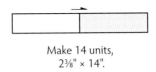

Make 14 units, 2⅜" × 14".

5. Sew a light small triangle to the right edge of a nine-patch unit. Sew a light large triangle to the top of the unit. Make 14 units.

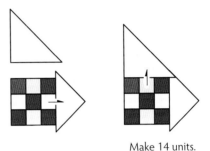

Make 14 units.

6. Sew a light 2⅜" × 7¼" rectangle to the left edge of a unit from step 5. Add a light large triangle. Make 14 units.

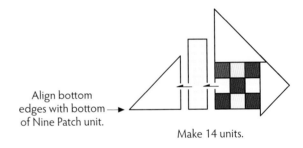

Align bottom edges with bottom of Nine Patch unit.

Make 14 units.

7. To make a half block, join the units from steps 3, 4, and 6, noting the orientation of the units and aligning the center seams. Make 14 half blocks.

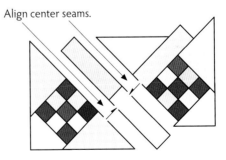

Align center seams.

Make 14 half blocks.

8. Trim each half block, making sure to leave ¼" seam allowance beyond the points of the nine-patch unit along the side and bottom edges. The blocks should measure 8¼" × 16", including seam allowances.

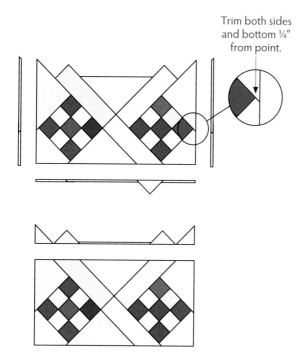

Trim both sides and bottom ¼" from point.

Trim each block to 8¼" × 16".

Making the Sashing Strips

1. Join two nine-patch units and two light 3¾" × 5" rectangles to make a vertical sashing strip. Make 16 strips measuring 5" × 16", including seam allowances.

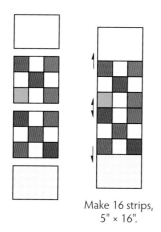

Make 16 strips,
5" × 16".

2. Join one nine-patch unit and one light 3¾" × 5" rectangle to make a partial sashing strip. Make eight strips measuring 5" × 8¼", including seam allowances.

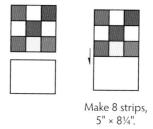

Make 8 strips,
5" × 8¼".

3. Join 12 nine-patch units and eight light 3¾" × 5" rectangles to make a horizontal sashing strip. Make five strips measuring 5" × 80½", including seam allowances.

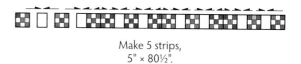

Make 5 strips,
5" × 80½".

Assembling the Quilt Top

1. Lay out two corner blocks, four partial sashing strips, and three half blocks, noting the orientation of the blocks and sashing strips. Join the pieces to make the top row. Repeat to make the bottom row. The rows should measure 8¼" × 80½", including seam allowances.

Top/bottom rows.
Make 2 rows, 8¼" × 80½".

2. Lay out two half blocks, four vertical sashing units, and three center blocks, noting the orientation of the half blocks. Join the pieces to make a center row. Make four rows measuring 16" × 80½", including seam allowances.

Center row.
Make 4 rows, 16" × 80½".

3. Lay out the top/bottom rows, center rows, and horizontal sashing rows, making sure to rotate the bottom row as shown in the quilt assembly diagram below. Join the rows. The quilt top should measure 80½" × 100½".

Finishing the Quilt

1. Layer the backing, batting and quilt top; baste the layers together.

2. Quilt by hand or machine. Lissa's quilt is machine quilted with allover converging spirals.

3. Use the dark red 2½"-wide strips to make binding and then attach the binding to the quilt.

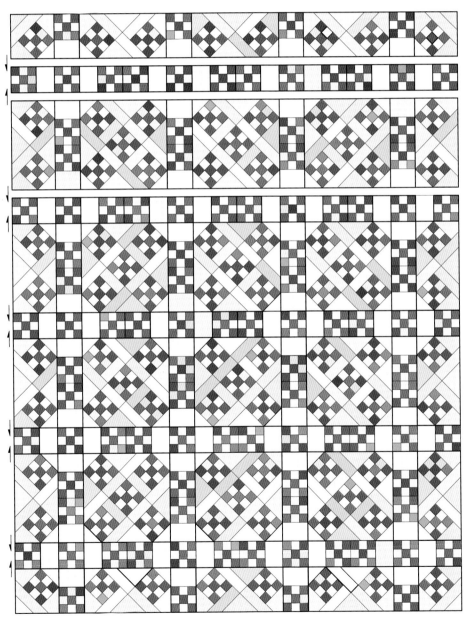

Quilt assembly

SCRAPPY DOTS AND DASHES

Designed by Lisa Bongean

Lisa wanted to use a piece of every fabric she had designed for Moda (up to this point!) in her quilt. Her design is simple but effective in creating a colorful patchwork garden of fabrics. Some quilters like to cut their scraps into strips or squares to save for future scrap quilts. If you don't have a box of these leftovers, a good way to get a mix of colors is to cut a 2" strip from all the dark and light fat quarters in your stash and let them play happily together.

FINISHED QUILT: 60½" × 72½"

Materials

Yardage is based on 42"-wide fabric.

- 2⅜ yards *total* of assorted light prints for units
- 4 yards *total* of assorted medium and dark prints (referred to collectively as "dark") for units
- ⅝ yard of red print for binding
- 3¾ yards of fabric for backing
- 67" × 79" piece of batting

Cutting

All measurements include ¼" seam allowances.

From the assorted light prints, cut a *total* of:
640 squares, 2" × 2"

From the assorted dark prints, cut a *total* of:
304 rectangles, 2" × 5"
16 rectangles, 2" × 3½"
336 squares, 2" × 2"

From the red print, cut:
7 strips, 2½" × 42"

Lissa's Scrap School Tip

Lisa's quilt is a study in darks and lights. She sprinkled in a few medium-value fabrics throughout to add some interest. Did you squint? Did you notice what a pop of color the golden yellows and oranges make throughout this quilt? They're used sparingly but add so much sparkle to the quilt.

Assembling the Quilt Top

Press all seam allowances as indicated by the arrows.

1. Join a light square and a dark 2" × 5" rectangle to make a unit. Make 304 units measuring 2" × 6½", including seam allowances.

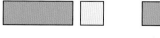

Make 304 units,
2" × 6½".

2. Join a light square and a dark square to make a unit. Make 320 units measuring 2" × 3½", including seam allowances.

Make 320 units,
2" × 3½".

3. Join a light square and a dark 2" × 3½" rectangle to make a unit. Make 16 units measuring 2" × 5", including seam allowances.

Make 16 units,
2" × 5".

4. To make row A, join 10 units from step 1, noting the orientation of the units. Make 16 rows measuring 2" × 60½", including seam allowances.

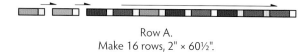

Row A.
Make 16 rows, 2" × 60½".

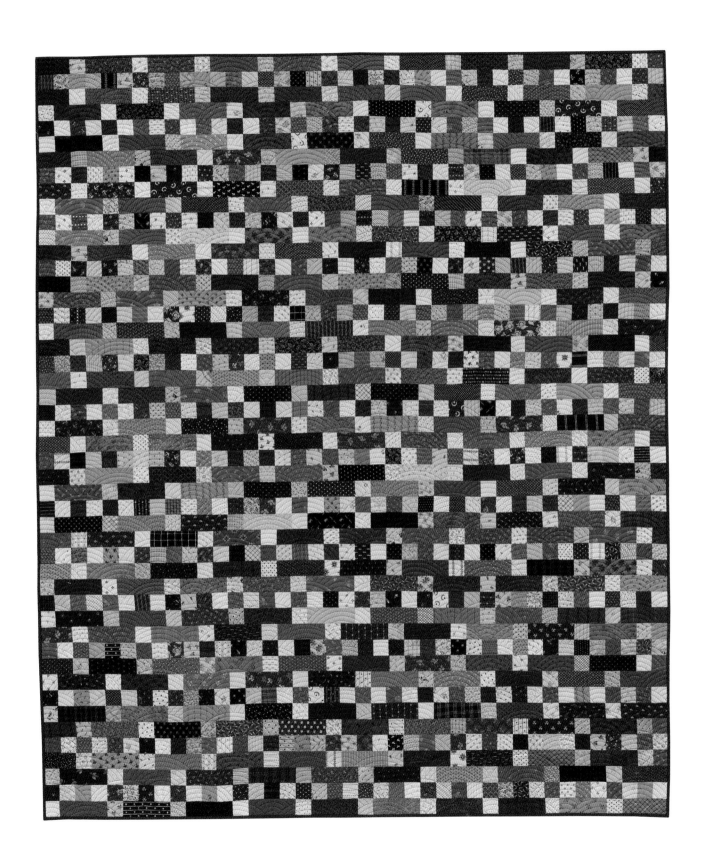

5. To make row B, join 20 units from step 2, noting the orientation of the units. Make 16 rows measuring 2" × 60½", including seam allowances.

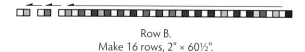

Row B.
Make 16 rows, 2" × 60½".

6. To make row C, join nine units from step 1, one unit from step 3, and one dark square. Make 16 rows measuring 2" × 60½", including seam allowances.

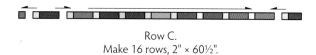

Row C.
Make 16 rows, 2" × 60½".

7. Lay out rows A–C as shown in the quilt assembly diagram below, repeating the sequence of the first six rows. Join the rows. The quilt top should measure 60½" × 72½".

Finishing the Quilt

1. Layer the backing, batting, and quilt top; baste the layers together.

2. Quilt by hand or machine. Lisa's quilt is machine quilted with an allover Baptist Fan design.

3. Use the red 2½"-wide strips to make binding, and then attach the binding to the quilt.

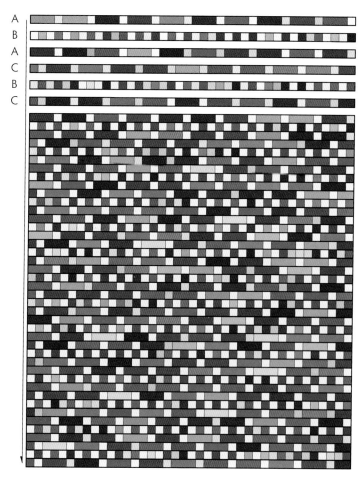

Quilt assembly

Color Option

I love plus sign quilts! For my color option of Scrappy Dots and Dashes, I played with fabrics that would make a fun baby quilt. Using an assortment of lights and pinks, I re-created Lisa's design by changing the value placement so the result looks like plus signs. My quilt is the same pattern but a different final product, all because of where I placed the darks and lights.

Stretch the range of pinks for a scrappy vintage feel. This pattern is a perfect scrap buster. Or use your favorite Jelly Roll strips.

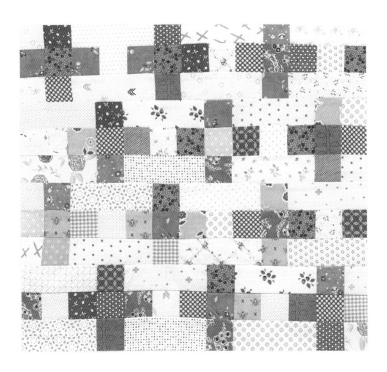

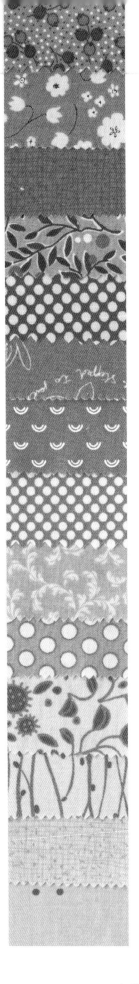

SEA GLASS STARS

Designed by Mary Etherington and Connie Tesene

Having been in business during the years when everything "country" was popular, Mary and Connie found working with a fresh new color palette very appealing. "We literally had to shop for new fabric in order to make this quilt. We also used a 60° triangle in our design, which is something we haven't used much. It made this quilt very fun!"

FINISHED QUILT: 79" × 79"

FINISHED BLOCK: 8¼" × 8¼"

- 87" × 87" piece of batting
- Template plastic (see "Optional Rulers" below)

Materials

Yardage is based on 42"-wide fabric.

- 4⅞ yards *total* of assorted blue, orange, aqua, and teal prints (referred to collectively as "dark") for blocks and border
- 4 yards *total* of assorted light prints for blocks
- 2⅓ yards of gray solid for sashing and binding
- ⅜ yard of orange print for cornerstones
- 7¼ yards of fabric for backing

Optional Supplies List

Instead of using template plastic to make templates for the A and B triangles, you can cut the required pieces using a Tri-Recs tool by Darlene Zimmerman. Another option would be Deb Tucker's V Block ruler.

Cutting

Before you begin cutting, trace patterns A and B on page 32 onto template plastic and cut them out. Use the templates to cut the A, A reversed, and B triangles from the fabrics indicated below. Each block contains one light and one dark fabric. Repeat the cutting instructions to make 32 light star units and 32 dark star units, keeping the fabrics for each unit together. All measurements include ¼" seam allowances.

FOR ONE LIGHT STAR UNIT

From 1 light print, cut:
4 of triangle A
4 of triangle A reversed
1 square, 2¼" × 2¼"

From 1 dark print, cut:
4 of triangle B
4 squares, 2¼" × 2¼"

FOR ONE DARK STAR UNIT

From 1 dark print, cut:
4 of triangle A
4 of triangle A reversed
1 square, 2¼" × 2¼"

From 1 light print, cut:
4 of triangle B
4 squares, 2¼" × 2¼"

FOR BLOCKS, SASHING, BORDER, AND BINDING

Before cutting the dark and light strips, see "Bits and Pieces" at right.

From the remaining assorted dark prints, cut a *total* of:
32 strips, 1½" × 5¾"
64 strips, 1½" × 6¾"
64 strips, 1½" × 7¾"
32 strips, 1½" × 8¾"
2¼"-wide rectangles in various lengths to total 325"

From the remaining assorted light prints, cut a *total* of:
32 strips, 1½" × 5¾"
64 strips, 1½" × 6¾"
64 strips, 1½" × 7¾"
32 strips, 1½" × 8¾"

From the gray solid, cut:
36 strips, 1½" × 42"; crosscut into 144 strips, 1½" × 8¾"
9 strips, 2½" × 42"

From the orange print, cut:
4 strips, 1½" × 42"; crosscut into 81 squares, 1½" × 1½"
4 squares, 2¼" × 2¼"

Bits and Pieces

To make the blocks extra scrappy, join 1½"-wide scraps and then cut the length of strips listed in "Cutting," keeping light and dark scraps separate.

Making the Blocks

Press all seam allowances as indicated by the arrows.

1. Sew matching light A and A reversed triangles to a dark B triangle to make a star-point unit measuring 2¼" square. Make 32 sets of four matching units, keeping like units together.

Make 32 sets of 4 matching units, 2¼" × 2¼".

Lissa's Scrap School Tip

Early in my quilting career, I used the phrase "clash factor" when I'd purposely use a color that didn't match the others. Back then I used it because I didn't want people to judge me. Now I use it intentionally because it's often what makes the quilt come to life. Connie and Mary used a pop of cheddar among all those cool colors to add the just right amount of pizzazz to their quilt. What colors would you add to your next project as a clash factor?

2. Lay out four matching star-point units from step 1, four matching dark squares, and one light square in three rows of three. The light and dark prints should match throughout. Sew the pieces into rows. Join the rows to make a light star unit. Make 32 units measuring 5¾" square, including seam allowances.

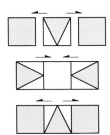
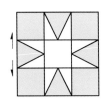

Make 32 light star units,
5¾" × 5¾".

3. Sew matching dark A and A reversed triangles to a light B triangle to make a star-point unit measuring 2¼" square, including seam allowances. Make 32 sets of four matching units, keeping like units together.

Make 32 sets of 4 matching units,
2¼" × 2¼".

4. Lay out four matching star-point units from step 3, four matching light squares, and one dark square in three rows of three. The light and dark prints should match throughout. Sew the pieces into rows. Join the rows to make a dark star unit. Make 32 units measuring 5¾" square, including seam allowances.

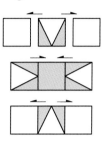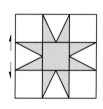

Make 32 dark star units,
5¾" × 5¾".

5. Sew a light 1½" × 5¾" strip to the right edge of a light star unit. Sew a light 1½" × 6¾" strip to the bottom and right edges of the unit. Continue adding light 1½"-wide strips as shown to make a block. Make 32 light Star blocks measuring 8¾" square, including seam allowances.

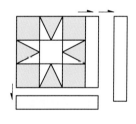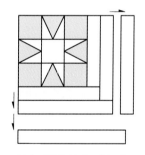

Make 32 light Star blocks,
8¾" × 8¾".

6. Repeat step 5 using the dark 1½"-wide strips and the dark star units. Make 32 dark Star blocks measuring 8¾" square, including seam allowances.

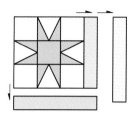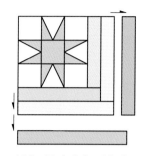

Make 32 dark Star blocks,
8¾" × 8¾".

Assembling the Quilt Top

1. Join nine orange 1½" squares and eight gray sashing strips to make a sashing row. Make nine rows measuring 1½" × 75½", including seam allowances.

Make 9 rows,
1½" × 75½".

2. Join nine gray sashing strips, four light blocks, and four dark blocks to make a row. Make eight rows measuring 8¾" × 75½", including seam allowances.

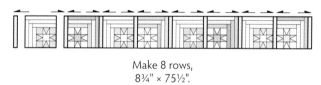

Make 8 rows,
8¾" × 75½".

3. Join the sashing rows and blocks rows as shown in the quilt assembly diagram on page 32, rotating every other block row 180°. The quilt-top center should measure 75½" square, including seam allowances.

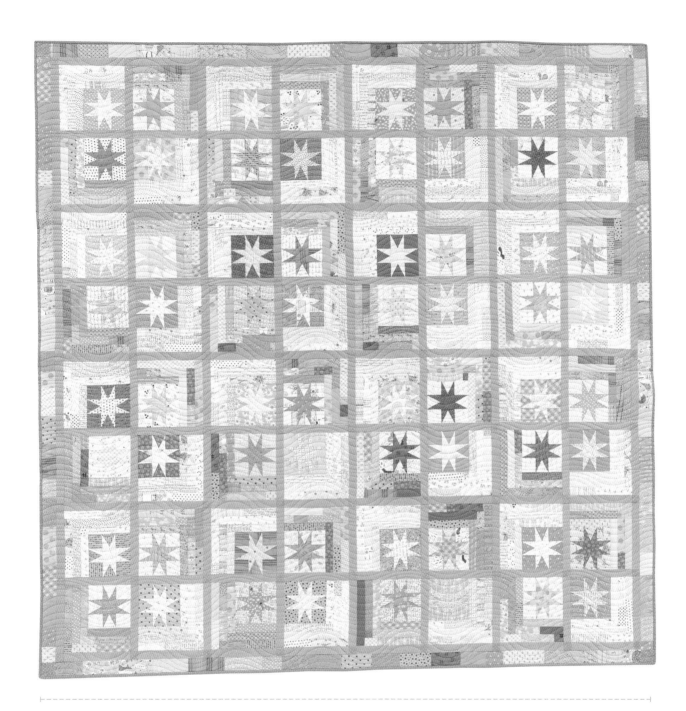

4. Join the dark 2¼"-wide rectangles end to end to make a pieced strip measuring approximately 325" long. From the pieced strip, cut four border strips, 2¼" × 75½". Sew orange 2¼" squares to the ends of two of the pieced strips for the top and bottom borders.

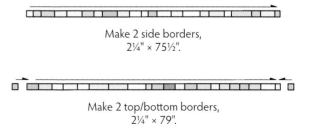

Make 2 side borders,
2¼" × 75½".

Make 2 top/bottom borders,
2¼" × 79".

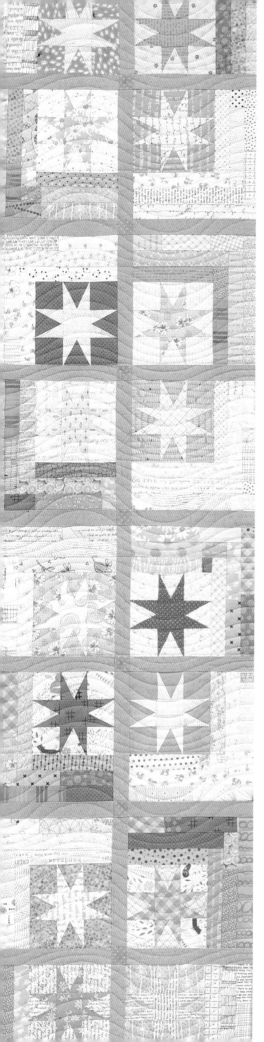

5. Sew the shorter borders to opposite sides of the quilt top and then add the top and bottom borders. The quilt top should measure 79" square.

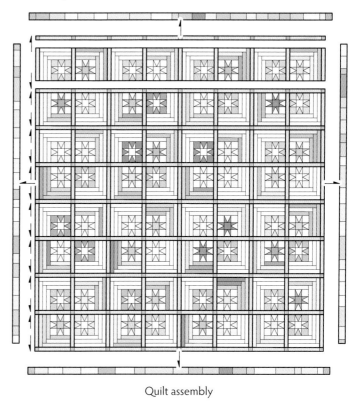

Quilt assembly

Finishing the Quilt

1. Layer the backing, batting, and quilt top; baste the layers together.

2. Quilt by hand or machine. Connie and Mary's quilt is machine quilted with an allover pattern of wavy lines.

3. Use the gray 2½"-wide strips to make binding, and then attach the binding to the quilt.

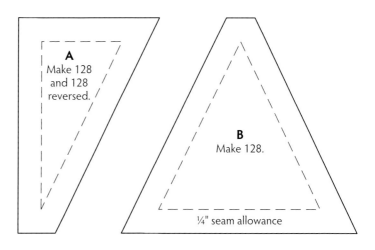

A
Make 128
and 128
reversed.

B
Make 128.

¼" seam allowance

Color Option

I chose a very traditional colorway for my color option for Sea Glass Stars, but wanted to focus on the light prints in my fabric swatch bar. One thing I love about fabric is how the values used can make the overall design recede or advance. Using a large variety of background prints instead of one light solid prevents the stronger main prints from standing out too much; the mix of light prints helps create a lower contrast. Mixing different shades of backgrounds from whites to creams and tans to taupes adds so much additional texture to the quilt. I intentionally shop for interesting background prints to add to my collection.

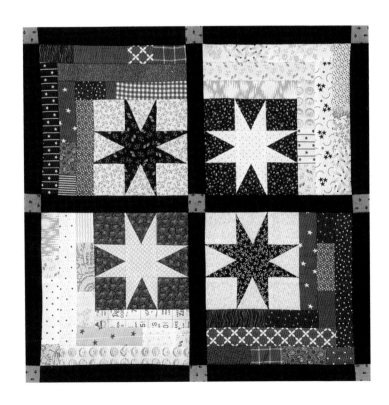

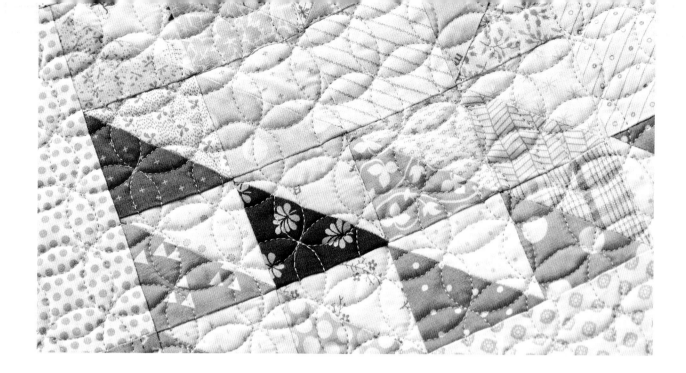

OMBRÉ BUTTERSCOTCH BASKETS

Designed and pieced by Lissa Alexander; quilted by Maggi Honeyman

Basket quilts are true classics. Quilters have developed so many styles of Basket blocks over the years. But vintage basket quilts are often stitched in just two or three colors. For a scrappy rendition, I wanted to use as many scraps as I could while paying homage to those earlier quilts. The result? I turned my two-color baskets into an ombré spectacular!

FINISHED QUILT: 71" × 85¼"

FINISHED BLOCK: 10" × 10"

Materials

Yardage is based on 42"-wide fabric.

- 4½ yards *total* of assorted light prints for blocks and setting triangles

- ¾ yard *total* of assorted pink and light orange prints for blocks

- ¾ yard *total* of assorted medium orange prints for blocks

- ¾ yard *total* of assorted dark orange and brown prints (referred to collectively as "brown") for blocks

- ⅓ yard *each* of 2 different orange prints for borders 1 and 3

- ⅝ yard *each* of 2 different light prints for borders 2 and 4

- ⅝ yard of brown print for border 5

- ⅝ yard of brown solid for binding

- 5¼ yards of fabric for backing

- 79" × 94" piece of batting

Cutting

All measurements include ¼" seam allowances.

From the assorted light prints, cut a *total* of:
64 rectangles, 2½" × 6½"

258 squares, 2⅞" × 2⅞"

96 squares, 2½" × 2½"

4 squares, 15½" × 15½"; cut the squares into quarters diagonally to yield 16 side triangles (2 are extra)

2 squares, 8" × 8"; cut the squares in half diagonally to yield 4 corner triangles

From the assorted pink and light orange prints, cut a *total* of:
86 squares, 2⅞" × 2⅞" (A)

From the assorted medium orange prints, cut a *total* of:
86 squares, 2⅞" × 2⅞" (B)

From the assorted brown prints, cut a *total* of:
86 squares, 2⅞" × 2⅞" (C)

From *each* of the orange prints for borders, cut:
8 strips, 1¼" × 42" (16 total)

From *each* of the light prints for borders, cut:
8 strips, 2½" × 42" (16 total)

From the brown print for border, cut:
8 strips, 2" × 42"

From the brown solid, cut:
8 strips, 2½" × 42"

Making the Blocks

Press all seam allowances as indicated by the arrows.

1. Draw a diagonal line from corner to corner on the wrong side of the light 2⅞" squares. Layer a marked square on an A square, right sides together. Sew ¼" from both sides of the drawn line. Cut the unit apart on the marked line to make two half-square-triangle units. Make 172 A units measuring 2½" square, including seam allowances.

Make 172 units,
2½" × 2½".

2. Repeat step 1 using the marked light squares and the B squares to make 172 B triangle units. Use the remaining marked squares and the C squares to make 172 C triangle units.

Make 172 of each unit,
2½" × 2½".

3. Lay out 14 A triangle units and two light 2½" squares in four rows of four. Sew the pieces into rows. Join the rows to make a basket unit. Make 10 units measuring 8½" square, including seam allowances.

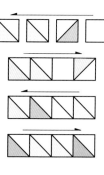 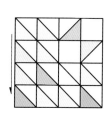

Make 10 units,
8½" × 8½".

4. Sew an A unit from step 1 to one end of a light rectangle to make a base unit. Repeat to make a second unit, orienting the A unit as shown. Make 10 of each unit. The base units should measure 2½" × 8½", including seam allowances.

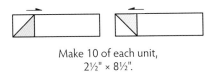

Make 10 of each unit,
2½" × 8½".

5. Lay out one basket unit, one of each base unit from step 4, and one light 2½" square as shown. Sew the pieces into rows. Join the rows to make an A block. Make 10 blocks measuring 10½" square, including seam allowances.

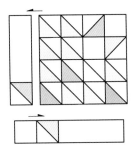
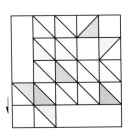

Block A.
Make 10 blocks,
10½" × 10½".

6. Repeat steps 3–5, using the B triangle units instead of the A units to make 10 B blocks. Use the C triangle units instead of the A units to make 10 C blocks.

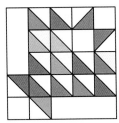
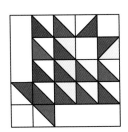

Block B.
Make 10 blocks,
10½" × 10½".

Block C.
Make 10 blocks,
10½" × 10½".

7. Repeat steps 3–5, using a combination of the remaining A and B triangle units to make one block. Use a combination of the remaining B and C triangle units to make another block. You'll have four triangle units left over for another project.

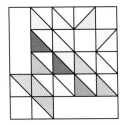
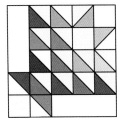

Make 1 of each block,
10½" × 10½".

Experiment with Color!

Making all-brown baskets would be boring; making all-orange baskets would be very bright. So I decided to create a cornucopia of color by letting the flow of color run from light to dark. This quilt was so much fun to make and I was able to work with little bits of color without any one color overpowering the quilt. Whether you choose to re-create an ombré look or make it totally scrappy, I encourage you to have fun with the basket elements. Twist and turn the triangles to create different baskets. And feel free to swap out some of the triangles for a plain square as I did in one of my blocks. Can you spy it?!

Assembling the Quilt Top

1. Lay out the blocks in diagonal rows as shown in the quilt assembly diagram below, placing A blocks at the top of the quilt, C blocks at the bottom, and the remaining blocks in between to create the ombré effect. Add the light side and corner triangles around the perimeter. Sew the blocks and side triangles into rows. Join the rows, adding the corner triangles last.

Quilt assembly

2. Trim and square up the quilt top, making sure to leave ¼" beyond the points of all blocks for seam allowances. The quilt-top center should measure 57" × 71¼", including seam allowances.

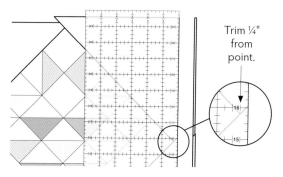

Trim ¼" from point.

Lissa's Scrap School Tip

Don't be afraid to push the boundaries with your color choices. Take a look at the close-up photo above and you'll see that I included red-browns that are almost burgundy with my browns, and butterscotch prints that aren't really orange. Stepping away from the expected will really make your quilt shine.

3. Referring to the adding borders diagram on page 41, join eight matching orange 1¼"-wide strips end to end. From the pieced strip, cut two 71¼"-long strips and two 58½"-long strips. Sew the longer strips to opposite sides of the quilt top. Sew the shorter strips to the top and bottom edges. The quilt top should measure 58½" × 72¾", including seam allowances.

4. Join eight matching light 2½"-wide strips end to end. From the pieced strip, cut two 72¾"-long strips and two 62½"-long strips. Sew the longer strips to opposite sides of the quilt top. Sew the shorter strips to the top and bottom edges. The quilt top should measure 62½" × 76¾", including seam allowances.

5. Join the remaining orange 1¼"-wide strips end to end. From the pieced strip, cut two 76¾"-long strips and two 64"-long strips. Sew the longer strips to opposite sides of the quilt top. Sew the shorter strips to the top and bottom edges. The quilt top should measure 64" × 78¼", including seam allowances.

6. Join the remaining light 2½"-wide strips end to end. From the pieced strip, cut two 78¼"-long strips and two 68"-long strips. Sew the longer strips to opposite sides of the quilt top. Sew the shorter strips to the top and bottom edges. The quilt top should measure 68" × 82¼", including seam allowances.

7. Join the brown print 2"-wide strips end to end. From the pieced strip, cut two 82¼"-long strips and two 71"-long strips. Sew the longer strips to opposite sides of the quilt top. Sew the shorter strips to the top and bottom edges. The completed quilt top should measure 71" × 85¼".

Finishing the Quilt

1. Layer the backing, batting, and quilt top; baste the layers together.

2. Quilt by hand or machine. Lissa's quilt is machine quilted with an allover egg and dart design.

3. Use the brown solid 2½"-wide strips to make binding, and attach the binding to the quilt.

Adding borders

COUNTY FAIR

Designed by Amy Smart; quilted by Melissa Kelley

Amy had a box of leftover 2½" squares, as well as a drawer full of "low-volume" (white background) print scraps, both waiting for just the right project. With this quilt she came up with a plan to use both! Country Fair is so fun to put together using favorite pieces left over from past projects. It's also a great one for showing off fussy-cut prints.

FINISHED QUILT: 63½" × 84¾"

FINISHED BLOCK: 6" × 6"

Materials

Yardage is based on 42"-wide fabric.

- 1⅜ yards *total* of assorted medium and dark prints (referred to collectively as "dark") for blocks

- ⅜ yard *total* of assorted light and medium prints (referred to collectively as "light") for blocks

- 3⅝ yards *total* of assorted white prints for blocks, sashing, and setting triangles

- ¼ yard of pink dot for cornerstones

- ⅓ yard of red dot for inner border

- 1⅛ yards of white solid for outer border

- ⅝ yard of red stripe for binding

- 5¼ yards of fabric for backing

- 72" × 93" piece of batting

Lissa's Scrap School Tip

Sometimes we spend so much time planning the scrappy fabrics for the main event that we forget that the background can be scrappy too. Amy's quilt is packed with punch, and much of that comes from the wide variety of low-volume prints she used for the background. Every last patch of this quilt deserves to be noticed!

Cutting

All measurements include ¼" seam allowances.

From the assorted dark prints, cut a *total* of:
236 squares, 2½" × 2½"

From the assorted light prints, cut a *total* of:
59 squares, 2½" × 2½"

From the assorted white prints, cut a *total* of:
236 squares, 2½" × 2½"
120 strips, 2" × 6½"
16 strips, 2" × 8½"
5 squares, 9¾" × 9¾"; cut the squares into
    quarters diagonally to yield 20 side triangles
2 squares, 7½" × 7½"; cut the squares in half
    diagonally to yield 4 corner triangles

From the pink dot, cut:
3 strips, 2" × 42"; crosscut into 58 squares, 2" × 2"

From the red dot, cut:
7 strips, 1½" × 42"

From the white solid, cut:
8 strips, 4½" × 42"

From the red stripe, cut:
8 strips, 2½" × 42"

Making the Blocks

Press all seam allowances as indicated by the arrows.

Lay out four dark squares from the same color family, four white 2½" squares, and one light 2½" square in three rows of three. Sew the squares into rows. Join the rows to make a block. Make 59 blocks measuring 6½" square, including seam allowances.

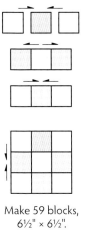

Make 59 blocks,
6½" × 6½".

Assembling the Quilt Top

1. Lay out the blocks, white 2" × 6½" strips, white 2" × 8½" strips, pink squares, and white side and corner triangles in diagonal rows, making sure to place the 2" × 8½" strips around the perimeter as shown in the quilt assembly diagram below. Sew the pieces into rows. Join the rows, adding the corner triangles last.

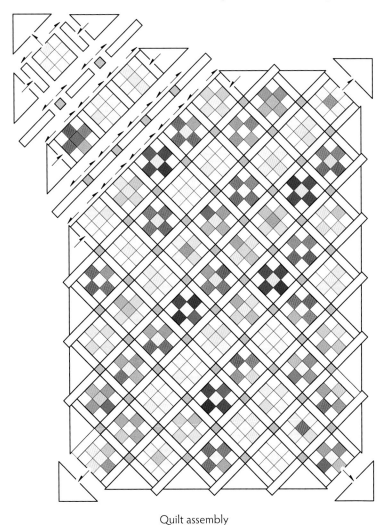

Quilt assembly

2. Trim and square up the quilt top, making sure to leave ¼" beyond the outer seam intersections for seam allowances. The quilt-top center should measure 53½" × 74¾", including seam allowances.

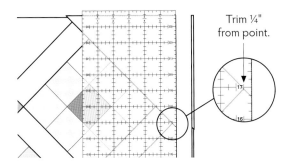

Trim ¼" from point.

3. Join the red 1½"-wide strips end to end. From the pieced strip, cut two 74¾"-long strips and two 55½"-long strips. Sew the longer strips to opposite sides of the quilt top. Sew the shorter strips to the top and bottom edges. The quilt top should measure 55½" × 76¾", including seam allowances.

Plan Ahead

Constancy in scrap quilts is sometimes overlooked, but that's not the case with Amy's quilt. The nine patches look like a field of patchwork flowers, but they're balanced with consistent setting triangles and sashing to ground the colors. Quite often scrap quilts are inspired from vintage styles and do not have borders. When a quilter ran out of fabric she was done. Here, adding the red border frames the quilt, and the additional wide border adds more visual interest to the inside of the quilt.

4. Join the white 4½"-wide strips end to end. From the pieced strip, cut two 76¾"-long strips and two 63½"-long strips. Sew the longer strips to opposite sides of the quilt top. Sew the shorter strips to the top and bottom edges. The quilt top should measure 63½" × 84¾".

Adding the borders

Finishing the Quilt

1. Layer the backing, batting, and quilt top; baste the layers together.

2. Quilt by hand or machine. Amy's quilt is machine quilted with an allover floral motif.

3. Use the red stripe 2½"-wide strips to make binding, and then attach the binding to the quilt.

TWO-STEP

Designed, pieced, and quilted by Amanda Jean Nyberg

Pair up fabrics from the same color family to make two-patch rectangles, then arrange them on a design wall and sew up your quilt! As with any scrap quilt, the more fabrics, the better. If you find you are lacking variety, swap fabric with a quilting friend or see the tip on page 50 for more ideas.

FINISHED QUILT: 60½" × 72½"

Materials

Yardage is based on 42"-wide fabric.

- 3 yards *total* of assorted light prints for blocks
- 3 yards *total* of assorted medium and dark prints (referred to collectively as "dark") for blocks
- ⅝ yard of gray stripe for binding
- 3¾ yards of fabric for backing
- 67" × 79" piece of batting

Cutting

All measurements include ¼" seam allowances.

From the assorted light prints, cut a *total* of:
540 squares, 2½" × 2½"

From the assorted dark prints, cut a *total* of:
540 squares, 2½" × 2½"

From the gray stripe, cut:
7 strips, 2½" × 42"

Lissa's Scrap School Tip

So simple, yet so clever: Amanda Jean's quilt looks at first glance like it's made of stacked rectangles, but all those rectangles are pieced from two same-color but different-fabric squares. She kept the palette clean and fresh, with aqua, lime, magenta, pink, orange, gray, and white as the main colors. What palette will you choose?

How to Make More Scraps

When it comes to scraps, Amanda Jean loves 2½" squares for their versatility. In fact, she has a drawer of them cut and ready at all times. If you don't have a supply of squares this size, you can supplement your scraps with precuts. Mini charm squares are just the right size and an inexpensive way to expand your selection. And don't forget about leftover pieces of 2½"-wide strips, which are perfect for crosscutting into squares.

Assembling the Quilt Top

Press all seam allowances as indicated by the arrows.

1. Join two light squares to make a light rectangle unit. Make 270 units measuring 2½" × 4½", including seam allowances.

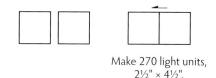

Make 270 light units, 2½" × 4½".

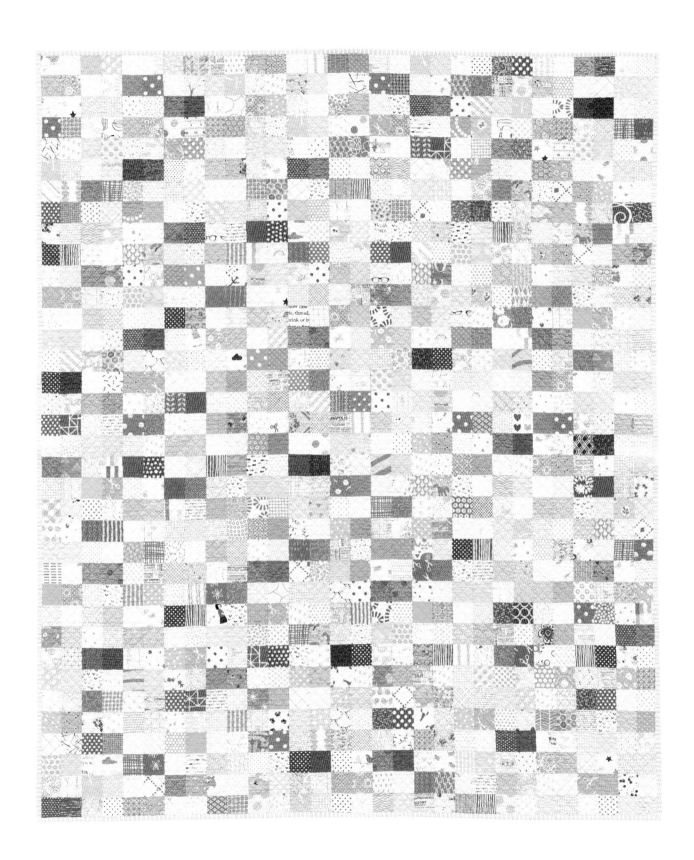

2. Join two dark squares from the same color family to make a dark rectangle unit. Make 270 units measuring 2½" × 4½", including seam allowances.

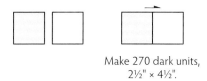

Make 270 dark units,
2½" × 4½".

3. Lay out the light and dark units in 36 rows of 15 units each, alternating the light and dark units in each row as shown in the quilt assembly diagram below. Sew the units into rows, and then join the rows. The quilt top should measure 60½" × 72½".

Finishing the Quilt

1. Layer the backing, batting, and quilt top; baste the layers together.

2. Quilt by hand or machine. Amanda Jean's quilt is machine quilted with an allover grid of diagonal lines.

3. Use the gray stripe 2½"-wide strips to make binding, and then attach the binding to the quilt.

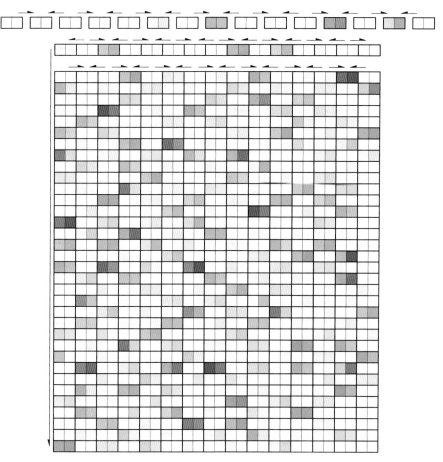

Quilt assembly

Color Option

I love the simplicity of this quilt pattern and rainbow colorway. It's a true color play and scrap buster that is perfect in any choice of fabric combinations. This quilt will be a good go-to pattern for anyone on your gift-giving list, from baby to graduate. Or maybe even for yourself!

This quilt pattern would make a great signature quilt or I SPY quilt. Choose the light areas to add family signatures as a precious keepsake for family reunions or a significant anniversary. The squares are big enough to fussy cut fabrics to create a sophisticated I SPY quilt with little treasures sprinkled throughout the blocks.

SPIN CYCLE

Designed and pieced by Gudrun Erla; quilted by Anne Hurlburt

If you love the look of scrap quilts but don't have an overflowing scrap basket, start with fat quarters like Gudrun did. For an even scrappier look, choose six different colors for the dark fat quarters instead of six different navy blues.

- -

FINISHED QUILT: 69½" × 95"

FINISHED BLOCKS: 13½" × 10½",
14¼" × 10½", and 7½" × 10½"

Materials

Yardage is based on 42"-wide fabric. Fat quarters measure 18"×21".

- 32 fat quarters of assorted light and medium prints (referred to collectively as "light") for blocks

- 7 fat quarters of assorted navy prints for blocks

- ¾ yard of navy print for binding

- 5¾ yards of fabric for backing

- 78" × 103" piece of batting

Cutting

All measurements include ¼" seam allowances.

From the assorted light prints, cut a *total* of:
27 strips, 2" × 21"
18 strips, 5" × 21"
180 rectangles, 2" × 3½"
41 rectangles, 5" × 8"
80 rectangles, 2" × 11"
10 rectangles, 2¾" × 11"
16 rectangles, 2" × 5"
8 rectangles, 3½" × 8"

From the assorted navy prints, cut a *total* of:
36 strips, 2" × 21"
16 squares, 2" × 2"

From the navy print for binding, cut:
9 strips, 2½" × 42"

Making the A and B Blocks

Press all seam allowances as indicated by the arrows.

1. Join a light 2" × 21" strip and a navy 2" × 21" strip to make a strip set. Make 27 strip sets measuring 3½" × 21", including seam allowances. Crosscut the strip sets into 270 segments, 2" × 3½".

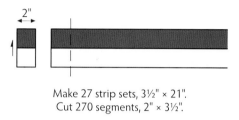

Make 27 strip sets, 3½" × 21".
Cut 270 segments, 2" × 3½".

2. Sew a light 5" × 21" strip to each long side of a navy 2" × 21" strip to make a strip set. Make nine strip sets measuring 11" × 21", including seam allowances. Crosscut the strip sets into 82 segments, 2" × 11".

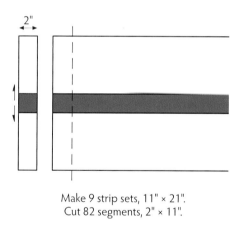

Make 9 strip sets, 11" × 21".
Cut 82 segments, 2" × 11".

3. Sew a segment from step 1 to a light 2" × 3½" rectangle to make a unit. Make 180 units measuring 3½" square, including seam allowances.

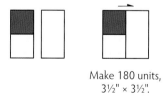

Make 180 units,
3½" × 3½".

4. Join two units from step 3 and one segment from step 1, noting the orientation of the units. Make 90 side units measuring 3½" × 8", including seam allowances.

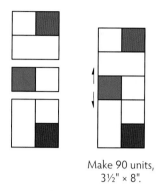

Make 90 units,
3½" × 8".

5. Sew side units from step 4 to opposite sides of a light 5" × 8" rectangle, noting orientation of the units. Make 41 units measuring 8" × 11", including seam allowances. Set aside the remaining units from step 4 for block C.

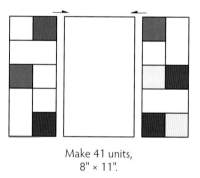

Make 41 units,
8" × 11".

6. Sew segments from step 2 to the top and bottom of a unit from step 5 to make a center unit. Make 41 units measuring 11" square, including seam allowances.

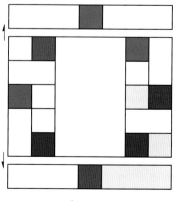

Make 41 units,
11" × 11".

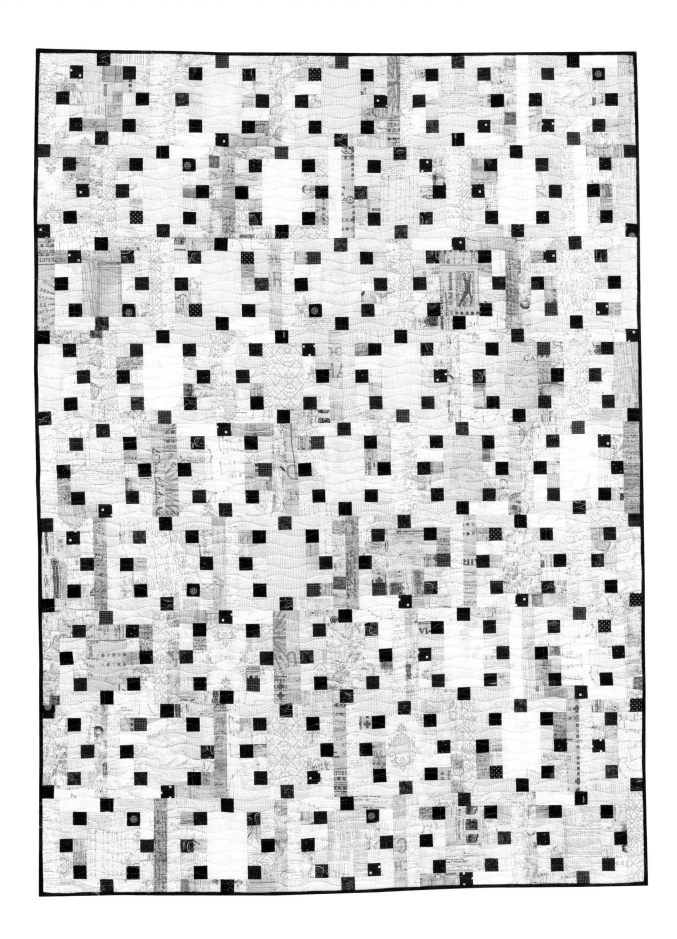

Lissa's Scrap School Tip

Spin Cycle makes good use of leftover strips, yet it also has a large piece in each block—perfect for using bigger-scale prints. Gudrun shows how you can mix background prints of different shades and with variation in their values to good success. The common thread these prints share is that they're all similar in scale, helping to maintain overall balance.

---

7. Sew light 2" × 11" rectangles to opposite sides of a center unit to make block A. Make 31 blocks measuring 11" × 14", including seam allowances.

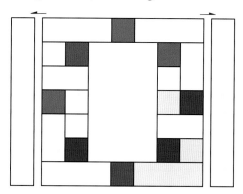

Block A.
Make 31 blocks,
11" × 14".

8. Sew a light 2" × 11" rectangle to one side and a light 2¾" × 11" rectangle to the opposite side of a remaining center unit to make block B. Make 10 blocks measuring 11 × 14¾", including seam allowances.

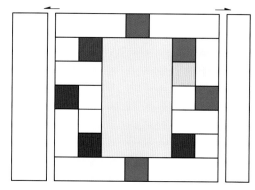

Block B.
Make 10 blocks,
11" × 14¾".

Making the C Blocks

1. Sew a navy 2" square to one end of a light 2" × 5" rectangle. Make 16 units measuring 2" × 6½", including seam allowances.

Make 16 units,
2" × 6½".

2. Sew a side unit from step 4 of "Making the A and B Blocks" to a light 3½" × 8" rectangle, noting the orientation of the unit. Make eight units measuring 6½" × 8", including seam allowances.

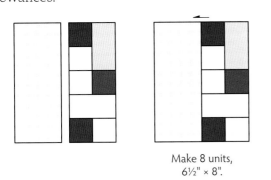

Make 8 units,
6½" × 8".

3. Sew units from step 1 to the top and bottom edges of a unit from step 2. Make eight units measuring 6½" × 11", including seam allowances.

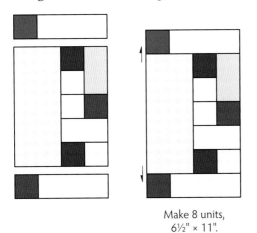

Make 8 units,
6½" × 11".

4. Sew a light 2" × 11" rectangle to the right edge of a unit from step 3 to make block C. Make eight blocks measuring 8" × 11", including seam allowances.

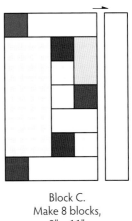

Block C.
Make 8 blocks,
8" × 11".

Assembling the Quilt Top

1. Join three A blocks and two B blocks to make a row, placing the wider rectangle on the B blocks along the outer edges. Make five rows measuring 11" × 69½", including seam allowances.

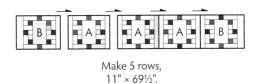

Make 5 rows,
11" × 69½".

2. Join four A blocks and two C blocks to make a row, placing the longest rectangle on the C blocks next to an A block. Make four rows measuring 11" × 69½", including seam allowances.

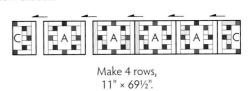

Make 4 rows,
11" × 69½".

3. Join the rows from steps 1 and 2, alternating them as shown in the quilt assembly diagram below. The quilt top should measure 69½" × 95".

Finishing the Quilt

1. Layer the backing, batting, and quilt top; baste the layers together.

2. Quilt by hand or machine. Gudrun's quilt is machine quilted with an allover pattern of wavy lines.

3. Use the navy 2½"-wide strips to make binding, and then attach the binding to the quilt.

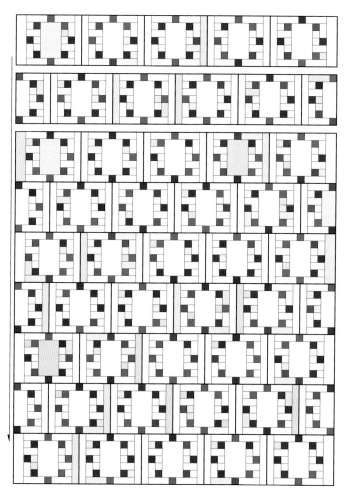

Quilt assembly

Color Option

For my color option, I really switched things up. First, I swapped the dark and light values, using darks for the larger pieces rather than lights and mediums. Then, I chose batiks. I don't often work with batiks, but they all seem to go nicely together so I thought this was the perfect pattern to try them out. I wanted a colorway that was inspired by the landscape of Hawaii. Mixing blues, aquas, greens, and a touch of purple for the background with a pop of hot pink to represent the lush flowers really puts me in an island mood.

WHILE AT LUNCH

Designed, pieced, and quilted by Sarah Huechteman

Quilting inspiration is everywhere—even underfoot. A bold tile pattern in a restaurant caught designer Sarah's eye while she was out for lunch, and before her family knew it, she was snapping pictures of the floor. Her colorful interpretation of the original black-and-white design creates a fun modern quilt.

FINISHED QUILT: 64½" × 80½"

FINISHED BLOCK: 8" × 8"

Materials

Yardage is based on 42"-wide fabric.

- 4½ yards *total* of assorted light prints for blocks
- 3¾ yards *total* of assorted turquoise prints for blocks and binding
- 1½ yards *total* of assorted gray prints for blocks
- 4⅞ yards of fabric for backing
- 71" × 87" piece of batting

Cutting

All measurements include ¼" seam allowances.

From the assorted light prints, cut a *total* of:
40 squares, 9" × 9"
80 squares, 4½" × 4½"

From the assorted turquoise prints, cut a *total* of:
40 squares, 9" × 9"
15 strips, 2½" × 21"

From the assorted gray prints, cut a *total* of:
80 squares, 4½" × 4½"

Making the Blocks

Press all seam allowances as indicated by the arrows.

1. Draw a diagonal line from corner to corner on the wrong side of the light 9" squares. Layer a marked square on a turquoise square, right sides together. Sew ¼" from both sides of the drawn line. Cut the unit apart on the marked line to make two half-square-triangle units. Trim the units to measure 8½" square, including seam allowances. Make 80 units.

Make 80 units.

2. Draw a diagonal line from corner to corner on the wrong side of the light 4½" squares and gray 4½" squares. Place a marked light square on the turquoise corner of a half-square-triangle unit, right sides together, and noting the orientation of the line. Sew on the marked line. Trim the excess corner fabric, ¼" from the stitched line. Repeat with a marked gray square on the opposite corner of the unit as shown to make a block. Make 80 blocks measuring 8½" square, including seam allowances.

Make 80 blocks,
8½" × 8½".

Extra Credit—Pillows!

To put every bit of your fabric to use, try this tip from Sarah. After stitching the marked light square on the corner of each block, *don't* trim the excess corner fabric. Instead, stitch a second line ½" from the first one, toward the corner. Cut between the two stitched lines and set aside the corner section. Repeat with the marked gray squares. Trim the resulting half-square-triangle units to measure 3" square, including seam allowances. You'll have enough bonus units to make two 20" pillows.

Lissa's Scrap School Tip

Sarah's design is essentially two colors—aqua and gray. Using several fabrics of each color adds movement and depth, creating a three-dimensional design. The pieces are bigger than some of the other quilts in this book, so it's easy to incorporate large-scale prints. Imagine making this quilt in school colors: perfect for your favorite grad!

Assembling the Quilt Top

Lay out the blocks in 10 rows of eight blocks each, rotating every other block 90° as shown in the quilt assembly diagram at right. Sew the blocks into rows, and then join the rows. The quilt top should measure 64½" × 80½".

Finishing the Quilt

1. Layer the backing, batting, and quilt top; baste the layers together.

2. Quilt by hand or machine. Sarah's quilt is machine quilted with an allover egg and dart design.

3. Use the turquoise 2½"-wide strips to make binding, and then attach the binding to the quilt.

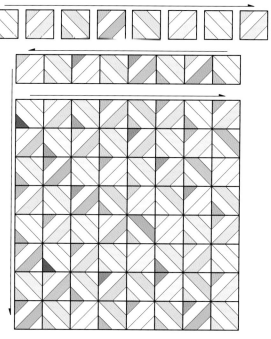

Quilt assembly

Color Option

I had a hard time creating a color option for this quilt because I loved everything about it and wanted to copy it exactly! I took a picture of the quilt with my phone and converted the photo to black and white so I could concentrate only on value (how dark or light the fabrics are), rather than on the specific colors.

Then I chose some leftovers from a Layer Cake to use as my color palette, which gave me confidence to pull additional fabrics to add to the final project. Notice, too, how I was able to make good use of large-scale prints in the bigger pieces of this design.

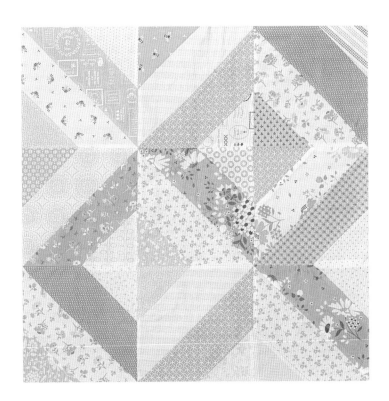

IT ALL ADDS UP

Designed by Susan Ache; quilted by Susan Rodgers

Plus Signs and Snowballs—it's hard to choose a favorite block, so Susan combined two of her favorites into one. Take a cue from Susan and stitch these combo blocks in as many reds and blues as you can. Notice that she didn't limit her colors to just one value. She used dark blues, light blues, and bright blues. I promise, it will all add up to FUN!

FINISHED QUILT: 65½" × 80½"

FINISHED BLOCKS: 7½" × 7½" and 5" × 5"

Materials

Yardage is based on 42"-wide fabric.

- 5⅜ yards *total* of assorted medium and dark blue prints for blocks
- 5 yards *total* of assorted light prints for blocks
- 1 yard *total* of assorted red prints for blocks
- 1 yard of red print for inner border and binding
- 5 yards of fabric for backing
- 74" × 89" piece of batting

Cutting

Each center block contains one blue, one light, and one red fabric. Repeat the cutting instructions to make 63 center blocks. Each border block contains one blue and one light fabric. Repeat the cutting instructions to make 54 border blocks. All measurements include ¼" seam allowances.

FOR ONE CENTER BLOCK

From the assorted blue prints, cut:
2 squares, 2½" × 2½"
2 rectangles, 2" × 8"
2 rectangles, 2" × 5"

Continued on page 70

Continued on page 70

Continued from page 69

From the assorted light prints, cut:

2 squares, 2½" × 2½"

1 strip, 1¼" × 10"

4 squares, 3" × 3"

From the assorted red prints, cut:

1 strip, 1¼" × 10"

1 square, 2" × 2"

FOR ONE BORDER BLOCK

From the assorted blue prints, cut:

2 rectangles, 2" × 5½"

2 rectangles, 2" × 2½"

4 squares, 1" × 1"

From the assorted light prints, cut:

4 squares, 2" × 2"

1 square, 2½" × 2½"

FOR INNER BORDER AND BINDING

From the red print, cut:

7 strips, 1¾" × 42"

8 strips, 2½" × 42"

Making the Center Blocks

Each block uses one blue, one light, and one red print. Instructions are for making one block. Press all seam allowances as indicated by the arrows.

1. Draw a diagonal line from corner to corner on the wrong side of two light 2½" squares. Layer a marked square on a blue square, right sides together. Sew ¼" from both sides of the drawn line. Cut the unit apart on the marked line to make two half-square-triangle units. Trim the units to measure 2" square, including seam allowances. Make four units.

Make 4 units.

2. Join a red strip and a light strip to make a strip set measuring 2" × 10", including seam allowances. Crosscut the strip set into four segments, 2" square.

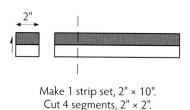

Make 1 strip set, 2" × 10".
Cut 4 segments, 2" × 2".

3. Lay out the units from step 1, the segments from step 2, and a matching red 2" square in three rows, noting the orientation of the units. Sew the pieces into rows. Join the rows to make a center unit measuring 5" square, including seam allowances.

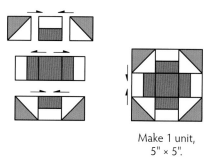

Make 1 unit,
5" × 5".

4. Sew blue 2" × 5" rectangles to opposite sides of the center unit. Sew blue 2" × 8" rectangles to the top and bottom edges to make a unit measuring 8" square, including seam allowances.

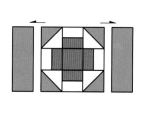 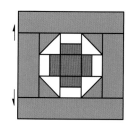

Make 1 unit,
8" × 8".

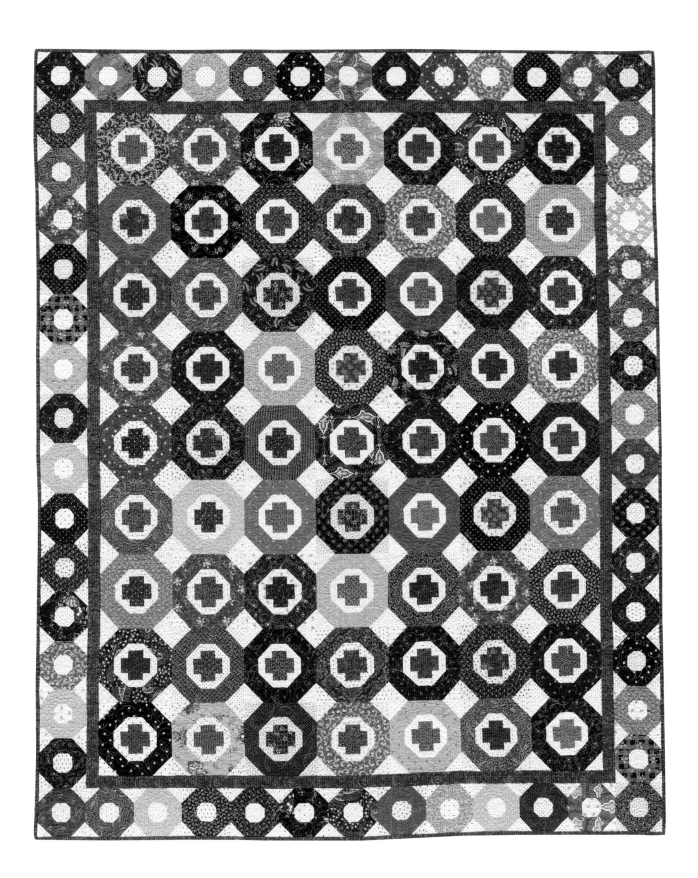

5. Draw a diagonal line from corner to corner on the wrong side of four light 3" squares. Place a marked square on each corner of the unit from step 4, right sides together, noting the orientation of the lines. Sew on the marked lines. Trim the excess corner fabric ¼" from the stitched lines. Repeat the steps to make a total of 63 center blocks measuring 8" square, including seam allowances.

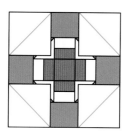 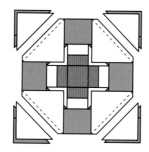

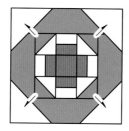

Center block.
Make 63 blocks, 8" × 8".

Making the Border Blocks

Each block uses one light and one blue print. Instructions are for making one block.

1. Draw a diagonal line from corner to corner on the wrong side of four light 2" squares. Layer marked squares on each end of a blue 2" × 5½" rectangle, right sides together. Sew on the marked lines. Trim the excess corner fabric ¼" from the stitched lines. Make two units measuring 2" × 5½", including seam allowances.

Make 2 units, 2" × 5½".

2. Draw a diagonal line from corner to corner on the wrong side of four blue 1" squares. Place marked squares on each corner of the light 2½" square. Sew on the marked line. Trim the excess corner fabric ¼" from the stitched lines. Make one snowball unit measuring 2½" square, including seam allowances.

Make 1 unit,
2½" × 2½".

3. Lay out the units from step 1, the snowball unit, and two blue 2" × 2½" rectangles in three rows. Join the rectangles and snowball unit to make the center row. Join the rows to make a block. Make 54 border blocks measuring 5½" square, including seam allowances.

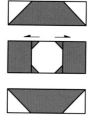

Border block.
Make 54 blocks,
5½" × 5½".

Background "Bench" Players

Even the pros count on those ball players sitting on the bench to be good supporting teammates. Susan did just that with her scrappy mix of lights used in the background. Why depend on a single background fabric when you can get scrappy!

Lissa's Scrap School Tip

Susan Ache's favorite season is summer and she gets to experience it all year long living in Florida. This red-white-and-blue quilt is perfect for Memorial Day, Fourth of July picnics, Labor Day, or donating to Quilts of Valor. To change it up, pick your two main colors and then stretch the range of shades to make the quilt sparkle.

Making the Outer Border

1. Join 14 border blocks to make a side border. Make two borders measuring 5½" × 70½", including seam allowances.

Make 2 side borders,
5½" × 70½".

2. Join 13 border blocks to make the top border. Repeat to make the bottom border. The borders should measure 5½" × 65½", including seam allowances.

Make 2 top/bottom borders,
5½" × 65½".

Assembling the Quilt Top

1. Lay out the center blocks in nine rows of seven blocks each as shown in the quilt assembly diagram below. Sew the blocks into rows, and then join the rows. The quilt-top center should measure 53" × 68", including seam allowances.

2. Join the red 1¾" × 42" strips end to end. From the pieced strip, cut two 68"-long strips and two 55½"-long strips. Sew the longer strips to opposite sides of the quilt top. Sew the shorter strips to the top and bottom edges. The quilt top should measure 55½" × 70½", including seam allowances.

3. Sew the side outer borders to opposite sides of the quilt top, and then add the top and bottom outer borders. The quilt top should measure 65½" × 80½".

Finishing the Quilt

1. Layer the backing, batting, and quilt top; baste the layers together.

2. Quilt by hand or machine. Susan's quilt is machine quilted with an allover pattern of feathers, swirls, and circles.

3. Use the red 2½"-wide strips to make binding, and then attach the binding to the quilt.

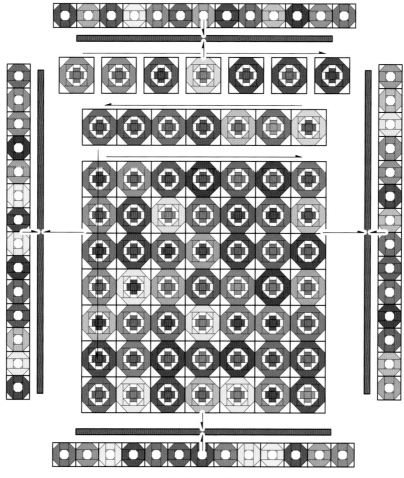

Quilt assembly

Color Option

I immediately thought of beach balls when I saw Susan's quilt. I used a colorful assortment of rainbow prints in a very scrappy layout to make my version of It All Adds Up. I don't know about you, but this version says "Summer School" to me!

CHARMING

Designed and pieced by Sherri L. McConnell

Sherri says, "I love the enticing mix of scrappy patchwork and decided to gather mini charms from a variety of fabric collections to begin making blocks. After finishing my quilt, I had the crazy idea that I might need to keep making more blocks for a king-size quilt!" Can you blame her?

FINISHED QUILT: 76⅝" × 76⅝"

FINISHED BLOCK: 9" × 9"

Materials

Yardage is based on 42"-wide fabric.

- 3¾ yards *total* of assorted light, medium, and dark prints (referred to collectively as "dark") for blocks*

- 1 yard of white print for blocks

*You can use one Moda Layer Cake of 42 precut 10" squares, one charm pack of 42 precut 5" squares, or four mini charm packs of 42 precut 2½" squares instead of the yardage listed.

- ⅞ yard of red print for cornerstones and binding

- 2¾ yards of cream tone on tone for sashing, setting triangles, and border

- 7 yards of fabric for backing

- 83" × 83" piece of batting

Cutting

All measurements include ¼" seam allowances.

From the assorted dark prints, cut a *total* of:

656 squares, 2½" × 2½"

From the white print, cut:

21 strips, 1½" × 42"; crosscut into 164 rectangles, 1½" × 4½"

Continued on page 78

Lissa's Scrap School Tip

Sherri used squares from all of her Moda collections, so the scraps play together nicely *and* form a great representation of her quilting life. Sometimes the beauty of making scrap quilts is the hum of the machine and the mindless therapy it offers. Sherri's quilt is a building block of shapes: make four patches, add cornerstones and sashing, then repeat.

Continued from page 77

From the red print, cut:

4 strips, 1½" × 42"; crosscut into 101 squares, 1½" × 1½"

8 strips, 2½" × 42"

From the cream tone on tone, cut:

25 strips, 1½" × 42"; crosscut into 100 rectangles, 1½" × 9½"

4 squares, 15½" × 15½"; cut the squares into quarters diagonally to yield 16 side triangles

2 squares, 8¾" × 8¾"; cut the squares in half diagonally to yield 4 corner triangles

8 strips, 2½" × 42"

Making the Blocks

Press all seam allowances as indicated by the arrows.

1. Lay out four dark squares in two rows of two. Sew the squares into rows. Join the rows to make a four-patch unit. Make 164 units measuring 4½" square, including seam allowances.

Make 164 units, 4½" × 4½".

2. Lay out four of the units from step 1, four white rectangles, and one red square in three rows. Sew the pieces into rows. Join the rows to make a block. Make 41 blocks measuring 9½" square, including seam allowances.

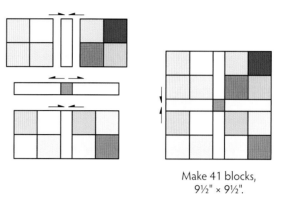

Make 41 blocks,
9½" × 9½".

Assembling the Quilt Top

1. Lay out the blocks, cream 1½" × 9½" rectangles, remaining red squares, and cream side and corner triangles in diagonal rows as shown in the quilt assembly diagram below. Join the cream strips and red squares to make sashing rows. Join the blocks and cream strips to make block rows. Sew a sashing row to the top or bottom of each adjacent block row and then add the side triangles. Join the rows, adding the corner triangles last.

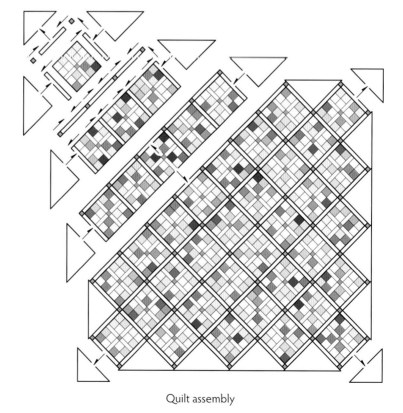

Quilt assembly

Check Your Work

One of the worst things when making scrap quilts is sewing two of the same fabrics together or close to each other, but building the quilt in units takes the guesswork out of where the fabrics will land. Make each four-patch unit with four distinctly different colors and then putting your quilt top together will be a breeze.

Sherri used two colors of sashing—one with a busier print to separate the four patches in each block and then a more subtle print to separate the large blocks from one another. This may seem unimportant, but this detail creates an extra level to the design, as the sashing looks like it's weaving in and out of the blocks. Adding a touch of your favorite color as the cornerstones throughout adds another level of design to play with.

2. Trim and square up the quilt top, making sure to leave ¼" beyond the points of all blocks for seam allowances. The quilt-top center should measure 72⅝" square, including seam allowances.

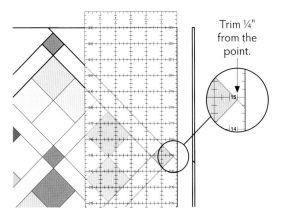

Trim ¼" from the point.

3. Join the cream 2½"-wide strips end to end. From the pieced strip, cut two 76⅝"-long strips and two 72⅝"-long strips. Sew the shorter strips to opposite sides of the quilt center. Sew the longer strips to the top and bottom edges. Press all seam allowances toward the border. The quilt top should measure 76⅝" square.

Finishing the Quilt

1. Layer the backing, batting, and quilt top; baste the layers together.

2. Quilt by hand or machine. Sherri's quilt is machine quilted with an allover Baptist Fan design.

3. Use the red 2½"-wide strips to make binding, and then attach the binding to the quilt.

HIDDEN BLOCKS

Designed and pieced by Lissa Alexander; quilted by Maggi Honeyman

Have you ever made a quilt that's so fun to sew that you wake up in the middle of the night just so you can squeeze in a few more hours of sewing before work? I have and this is the quilt. Learn more about this puzzle quilt on page 86!

FINISHED QUILT: 68⅜" × 76⅞"

FINISHED BLOCK: 6" × 6"

Materials

Yardage is based on 42"-wide fabric.

- 4¾ yards *total* of assorted light prints for blocks

- 4⅝ yards *total* of assorted medium and dark prints (referred to collectively as "dark A") for blocks

- ⅞ yard *total* of assorted light, medium, and dark prints (referred to collectively as "dark B") for setting triangles

- ⅝ yard of blue diagonal stripe for binding

- 4⅝ yards of fabric for backing

- 75" × 83" piece of batting

Cutting

All measurements include ¼" seam allowances.

From the assorted light prints, cut a *total* of:
128 pairs of squares, 3" × 3" (256 total)
128 strips, 1½" × 10½"
62 squares, 2½" × 2½"
6 sets of 4 matching squares, 2½" × 2½" (24 total)

From the dark A prints, cut a *total* of:
128 pairs of squares, 3" × 3" (256 total)
128 strips, 1½" × 10½"
66 squares, 2½" × 2½"

Continued on page 84

Continued from page 83

From the dark B prints, cut a *total* of:

8 squares, 9¾" × 9¾"; cut the squares into
    quarters diagonally to yield 32 side triangles
    (2 are extra)

2 squares, 5¼" × 5¼"; cut the squares in half
    diagonally to yield 4 corner triangles

From the blue stripe, cut:

8 strips, 2½" × 42"

Making the Blocks

Press all seam allowances as indicated by the
arrows.

1. Draw a diagonal line from corner to corner
on the wrong side of the light 3" squares. Layer
a marked square on a dark A 3" square, right
sides together. Sew ¼" from both sides of the
drawn line. Cut the unit apart on the marked
line to make two half-square-triangle units.
Trim the units to measure 2½" square, including
seam allowances. Make 128 sets of four
matching units.

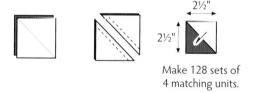

Make 128 sets of
4 matching units.

2. Join a light strip and a dark A strip to make
a strip set. Make 128 strip sets measuring
2½" × 10½", including seam allowances.
Crosscut each strip set into 4 segments,
2½" square, to yield 512 segments total.
Keep like segments together.

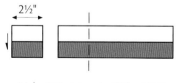

Make 128 strip sets, 2½" × 10½".
Cut 512 segments, 2½" × 2½".

3. Lay out four matching triangle units, four
matching segments, and one light 2½" square
in three rows, placing the light triangles and
rectangles along the outer edges. Join the
pieces to make a light Churn Dash block. Make
62 blocks measuring 6½" square.

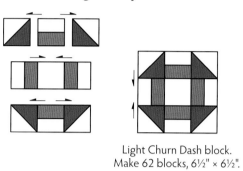

Light Churn Dash block.
Make 62 blocks, 6½" × 6½".

Mix It Up

To add another scrappy element, use a
dark 2½" square instead of a light center
square in a few of the light blocks.

4. Lay out four matching triangle units, four
matching segments, and one dark A 2½" square
in three rows, placing the dark triangles and
rectangles along the outer edges. Join the
pieces to make a dark Churn Dash block. Make
four blocks measuring 6½" square.

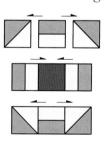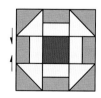

Dark Churn Dash block.
Make 4 blocks, 6½" × 6½".

Lissa's Scrap School Tip

I used a simple block, but experimented with the color placement to create a puzzle within a puzzle. I just couldn't wait to see what the next one would look like! Look closely—there are a few different blocks hidden in this puzzle, created just by omitting a piece from the original quilt block design. Whatever your color scheme, have fun with this puzzle, er, quilt.

5. Lay out four matching triangle units, four matching segments, and one dark A 2½" square in three rows, noting the orientation of the units. Sew the pieces into rows. Join the rows to make a Greek Cross block. Make 56 blocks measuring 6½" square, including seam allowances.

6. Lay out four matching triangle units, four matching light 2½" squares, and one dark A 2½" square in three rows. Sew the pieces into rows. Join the rows to make a Shoofly block. Make six blocks measuring 6½" square, including seam allowances.

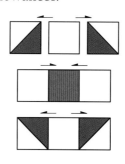

Shoo Fly block.
Make 6 blocks,
6½" × 6½".

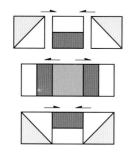
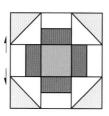

Greek Cross block.
Make 56 blocks,
6½" × 6½".

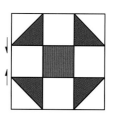

Assembling the Quilt Top

Lay out the Churn Dash blocks in an on-point grid of eight blocks by nine blocks, randomly placing a Shoofly block where you would have otherwise placed a Churn Dash block. Place a Greek Cross block between the Churn Dash blocks and the dark B side triangles around the outer edges as shown in the quilt assembly diagram below. Sew the pieces into diagonal rows. Join the rows, adding the corner triangles last. The quilt top should be 68⅜" × 76⅞".

Finishing the Quilt

1. Layer the backing, batting, and quilt top; baste the layers together.

2. Quilt by hand or machine. Lissa's quilt is machine quilted with an allover pattern of parallel wavy lines.

3. Use the blue stripe 2½"-wide strips to make binding, and then attach the binding to the quilt.

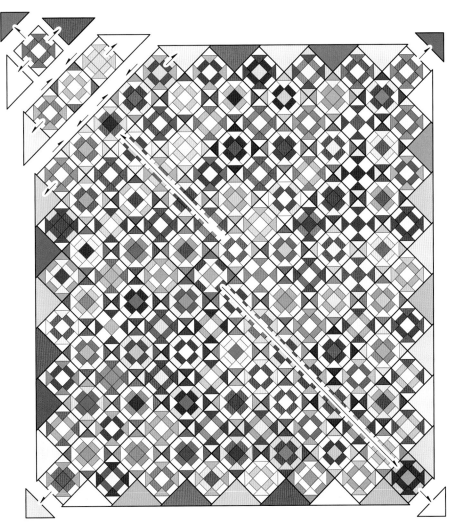

Quilt assembly

PLEASE AND THANK YOU

Designed and pieced by Kim Diehl; machine quilted by Connie Tabor

Taking a "more the merrier" approach when gathering assorted prints will produce blocks that truly sparkle—the key is choosing primarily medium and dark values for a strong sense of movement and balance in this ideal stash buster.

FINISHED QUILT: 60½" × 60½"

FINISHED BLOCK: 8" × 8"

Materials

Yardage is based on 42"-wide fabric. Chubby sixteenths measure 9"×10½". Bitty bricks measure 4½"×10½".

- 25 bitty bricks of assorted medium and dark prints (referred to collectively as "dark") for small churn-dash units and scrappy binding

- 25 chubby sixteenths of assorted medium and dark prints (referred to collectively as "dark") for large Star blocks and scrappy binding

- 1½ yards of tan print A for small churn-dash units and large Star and Churn Dash blocks

- 1¾ yards of cream print for large Star and Churn Dash blocks

- 24 bitty bricks of assorted medium and dark prints (referred to collectively as "dark") for small star units and scrappy binding

- ½ yard of tan print B for small star units

- 24 chubby sixteenths of assorted medium and dark prints (referred to collectively as "dark") for large Churn Dash blocks and scrappy binding

- ½ yard of black print for border

- 3¾ yards of fabric for backing

- 67" × 67" piece of batting

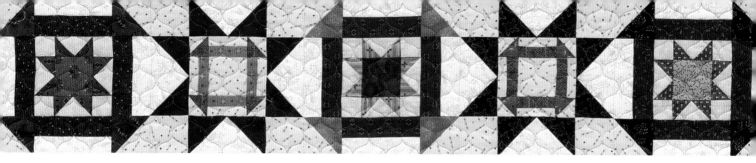

Cutting

All measurements include ¼" seam allowances.

From *each* of the 25 dark prints for small churn-dash units, cut:

1 strip, 1" × 10½" (25 total)
2 squares, 1⅞" × 1⅞" (50 total); cut the squares in half diagonally to yield 100 small triangles

Keep like pieces together for the small churn-dash units. Reserve the scraps for the binding.

From tan print A, cut:

9 strips, 1" × 42"; crosscut into 25 strips, 1" × 10½"
3 strips, 1⅞" × 42"; crosscut into 50 squares, 1⅞" × 1⅞". Cut the squares in half diagonally to yield 100 small triangles.
9 strips, 2½" × 42"; crosscut into 125 squares, 2½" × 2½"
4 strips, 2⅞" × 42"; crosscut into 48 squares, 2⅞" × 2⅞". Cut the squares in half diagonally to yield 96 large triangles.

From *each* of the 25 dark prints for large Star blocks, cut:

2 strips, 2½" × 10½"; crosscut into 8 squares, 2½" × 2½" (200 total)

Keep like pieces together for the large Star blocks. Reserve the scraps for the binding.

From the cream print, cut:

13 strips, 2½" × 42"; crosscut into 100 rectangles, 2½" × 4½"
16 strips, 1½" × 42"; crosscut into 48 strips, 1½" × 10½"

From *each* of the 24 dark prints for small star units, cut:

1 square, 2½" × 2½" (24 total)
8 squares, 1½" × 1½" (192 total)

Keep like pieces together for the small star units. Reserve the scraps for the binding.

From tan print B, cut:

10 strips, 1½" × 42"; crosscut into:
    96 rectangles, 1½" × 2½"
    96 squares, 1½" × 1½"

From *each* of the 24 dark prints for large Churn Dash blocks, cut:

2 strips, 1½" × 10½" (48 total)
1 strip, 2⅞" × 6½"; crosscut into 2 squares, 2⅞" × 2⅞" (48 total). Cut the squares in half diagonally to yield 96 triangles.

Keep like pieces together for the large Churn Dash blocks. Reserve the scraps for the binding.

From the black print, cut:

6 strips, 2½" × 42"

From the reserved assorted dark scraps, cut:

2½"-wide strips in various lengths to total 255"

Making the Small Churn-Dash Units

For each unit, you'll need four matching small triangles and one complementary dark strip from the pieces for the small churn-dash units. You'll also need the following tan A pieces: four small triangles, one strip, and one 2½" square. Instructions are for making one unit. Press all seam allowances as indicated by the arrows.

1. Sew together dark and tan triangles along their long edges. Press and trim off the dog-ear points. Make four half-square-triangle units measuring 1½" square, including seam allowances.

Make 4 units,
1½" × 1½".

2. Join a dark strip and a tan strip to make a strip set measuring 1½" × 10½", including seam allowances. Crosscut the strip set into four segments, 1½" × 2½".

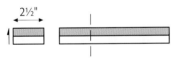

Make 1 strip set, 1½" × 10½".
Cut 4 segments, 1½" × 2½".

3. Lay out four triangle units, four segments, and one tan 2½" square in three rows. Sew the pieces into rows. Join the rows to make a churn-dash unit. Make a total of 25 units measuring 4½" square, including seam allowances.

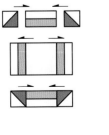

Make 25 units,
4½" × 4½".

Making the Large Star Blocks

1. Draw a diagonal line from corner to corner on the wrong side of eight matching dark 2½" squares for the large Star blocks. Place a marked square on one end of a cream 2½" × 4½" rectangle, right sides together. Sew on the marked line. Trim the excess corner fabric, ¼" from the stitched line. Place a marked square on the opposite end of the cream rectangle. Sew and trim as before to make a flying-geese unit. Make 25 sets of four matching units measuring 2½" × 4½", including seam allowances.

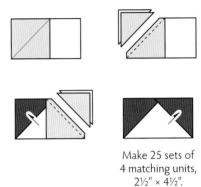

Make 25 sets of
4 matching units,
2½" × 4½".

2. Lay out four matching flying-geese units, four tan A 2½" squares, and one churn-dash unit. Sew the pieces into rows. Join the rows to make a large Star block. Make 25 blocks measuring 8½" square, including seam allowances.

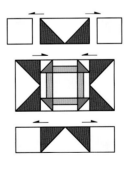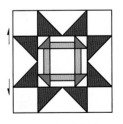

Large Star block
Make 25 blocks,
8½" × 8½".

Making the Small Star Units

1. Draw a diagonal line from corner to corner on the wrong side of eight matching dark 1½" squares for the small star units. Place a marked square on one end of a tan B rectangle, right sides together. Sew on the marked line. Trim the excess corner fabric, ¼" from the stitched line. Place a marked square on the opposite end of the tan rectangle. Sew and trim as before to make a flying-geese unit. Make 24 sets of four matching units measuring 1½" × 2½", including seam allowances.

Make 24 sets of
4 matching units,
1½" × 2½".

2. Lay out four flying-geese units, four tan B 1½" squares, and one dark 2½" square. Sew the pieces into rows. Join the rows to make a star unit. Make 24 units measuring 4½" square, including seam allowances.

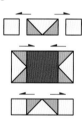

Make 24 units,
4½" × 4½".

Extra Credit—Mini Quilt

Quilt designer Kim says it's a snap to save and repurpose the scraps from Please and Thank You to make a bonus mini. Simply follow a few simple steps. Start by stitching the trimmed corner triangles from step 1 of "Making the Large Star Blocks" on page 91 into half-square-triangle units. Join the units into pinwheels and then trim them to 2½" square. With careful cutting in step 2 of "Making the Large Churn Dash Blocks" on page 94, you can end up with an extra 1½"-wide segment from the end of each strip set. Sew those segments together in matching pairs to make four-patch units measuring 2½" square. Add 2½" setting squares to your pinwheels and four patches, and then frame your finished quilt top with basic sashing and border strips. Fun, fast, and easy!

Making the Large Churn Dash Blocks

For each block, you'll need four matching dark triangles and two complementary dark strips from the pieces for the large Churn Dash blocks. You'll also need four tan A large triangles, two cream strips, and one star unit. Instructions are for making one block.

1. Sew together dark and tan triangles along their long edges. Press and trim off the dog-ear points. Make four half-square-triangle units measuring 2½" square, including seam allowances.

Make 4 units,
2½" × 2½".

Lissa's Scrap School Tip

You may not realize it immediately, but the background is doing a lot of the work in this design. Kim choose two light fabrics for the background and used them to guide your eye diagonally through the quilt. Alternating Churn Dash and Monkey Wrench blocks are each stitched in big and little versions. Squint to see how the background continues to work in the center of the small Churn Dashes. No wonder Kim named this quilt Please and Thank You—each of the blocks, much like the phrase, has great balance throughout.

2. Join a dark strip and a cream strip to make a strip set. Make two strip sets measuring 2½" × 10½", including seam allowances. Crosscut the strip sets into four segments, 2½" × 4½".

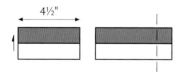

Make 2 strip sets, 2½" × 10½".
Cut 4 segments, 2½" × 4½".

3. Lay out four triangle units, four segments, and one star unit. Sew the pieces into rows. Join the rows to make a large Churn Dash block. Make 24 blocks measuring 8½" square, including seam allowances.

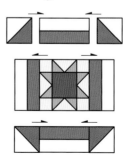
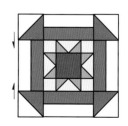

Large Churn Dash block
Make 24 blocks, 8½" × 8½".

Assembling the Quilt Top

1. Lay out the large Star and Churn Dash blocks in seven rows of seven blocks each, alternating them as shown in the quilt assembly diagram below. Sew the blocks into rows, and then join the rows. The quilt-top center should measure 56½" square, including seam allowances.

2. Join the black 2½"-wide strips end to end. From the pieced strip, cut two 60½"-long strips and two 56½"-long strips. Sew the shorter strips to opposite sides of the quilt center. Sew the longer strips to the top and bottom edges. The quilt top should measure 60½" square.

Finishing the Quilt

1. Layer the backing, batting, and quilt top; baste the layers together.

2. Quilt by hand or machine. Kim's quilt is machine quilted with an allover ogee lantern design.

3. Join the dark 2½"-wide strips of random lengths to make binding, and then attach the binding to the quilt.

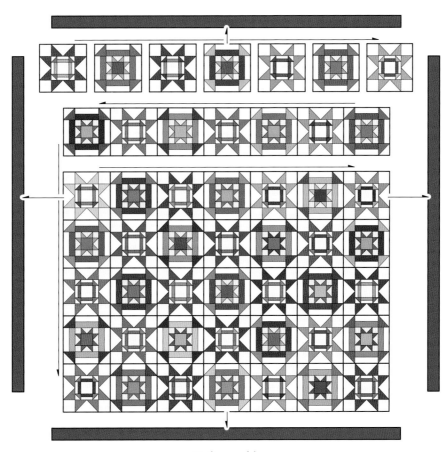

Quilt assembly

ABOUT THE AUTHOR

Lissa

**DEAN OF
SCRAP SCHOOL ADMISSIONS**

I've had a crazy, amazing life, a wild journey that I could never have imagined. Through it all, I've learned to take the pieces and stitch them together to make something new. My life is a patchwork of family, friends, and people who have made an impact.

My quilting story is a simple one. The first quilt I made was for a wedding gift. My sister and I worked on it together. It was a quilt-as-you-go project that we mailed back and forth between Lubbock and Dallas. It's clear that I was destined to be a scrap quilter because my next quilt was made from a sampler pack of a thousand 1½" squares. (I thought the finished quilt would be bigger.) My next quilt was made from "reading" the pictures in a Japanese magazine. I didn't realize the measurements were all metric, so needless to say, the second quilt was huge. You could say I am self-taught and continue to learn as I go.

The rest of my story is still a work in progress. It started with that first wedding quilt and led to working in a quilt shop. I raised kids and now I'm blessed with grandchildren. I am part of an industry and community of people who share my love for quilts and the people who make them.

My favorite thing about quilting is exploring color. Being good with color is all about practice—and using lots of it!

To everyone reading this, thank you for being part of my scrappy story.